GREAT ANSWERS, GREAT QUESTIONS FOR YOUR JOB INTERVIEW

SECOND EDITION

Jay A. Block & Michael Betrus

Mc
Graw
Hill
Education

New York   Chicago   San Francisco   Athens   London   Madrid
Mexico City   Milan   New Delhi   Singapore   Sydney   Toronto

1 2 3 4 5 6 7 8 9 0   QFR/QFR   1 2 0 9 8 7 6 5 4

ISBN 978-0-07-183774-3
MHID   0-07-183774-4

e-ISBN 978-0-07-183775-0
e-MHID   0-07-183775-2

Library of Congress Cataloging-in-Publication Data

Block, Jay A.
    Great answers, great questions for your job interview / by Jay A. Block and Michael Betrus. — 2nd edition.
        pages cm
    Includes bibliographical references.
    ISBN 978-0-07-183774-3 (alk. paper) — ISBN 0-07-183774-4 (alk. paper)
    1. Employment interviewing. I. Betrus, Michael. II. Title.
    HF5549.5.I6B564 2015
    650.14'4—dc23   2014011978

McGraw-Hill Education books are available at special quantity discounts to use as premiums and sales promotions or for use in corporate training programs. To contact a representative, please visit the Contact Us pages at www.mhprofessional.com.

Michael is dedicating this book to his son Michael, and Jay is dedicating this book to his son Ryco. We would also like to dedicate this to all our readers! There are so many terrific opportunities for everyone—here's hoping this helps you capture yours!

Contents

Part 3. After the Interview

Introduction

by Michael Betrus

SEVERAL YEARS AGO I was interviewing for a position as a regional director with a Fortune 50 telecommunications company. It was a big interview, representing the biggest job I'd had up to that time. The position had greater responsibility and higher compensation than any position I'd ever held. In short, this was a cherry opportunity and a terrific promotion.

Two days before the interview, preparation for the meeting was getting me very excited. I was traveling and was not able to prep as much as I normally would. On a plane from Baltimore to Tampa, I thought of the hiring I had done in the past. Then I put myself in the hiring vice president's mindset and began thinking about what would be important to her.

Put Yourself in the Hiring Manager's Mindset

What skills or accomplishments would be most important to this vice president? If I were in her shoes, what would be important to me in making a hiring decision? What would she ask me?

List It Out

Here is what I did. I anticipated several questions I thought she would ask and listed an answer to each one with a spin on what might be important to her. This is what the finished product looked like.

Strengths

- Good writing and communication skills (*I know this is vague, but it is always important, especially if you can back it, such as by being published or hosting seminars or training sessions.*)
- Ability to focus and see through the clutter (*along with a concise example to validate this*).
- Motivating a team to achieve success (*again accompanied by a concise example*).
- Effectively working across multiple disciplines in a large organization.
- Sense of urgency with deadlines, with examples to back it up.

Weaknesses

- Have a fairly direct personality (*a good weakness because it may be interpreted as a strength by some*).
- Have a difficult time working with those less passionate than I am (*again, a weakness that is forgivable*).
- Could sharpen Excel skills for better business analysis (*something easily done*).

Most Important Attributes to Me in a Job

- Being accountable and having the ability to affect the direction of the organization.
- Being able to win, to succeed.
- Creating an environment where employees can grow and enjoy their work.
- Developing a new business out of nothing, from staffing, training, development, and execution of a new business plan.
- Having passion and a sense of urgency to accomplish, a trait nearly impossible to teach.

Personnel Problem Solved

- Sharing office space with a sister business unit that was not "friendly." Morale issues arose, and I worked to bring harmony between the business units by:
    - Including both units in off-site team-building meetings.
    - Offering extra money for sales referrals and for assisting in special projects.

Skills to Develop

- Acquire more technical knowledge.

How You Set Priorities

- It begins and ends with the charter set by my management.
- I use a priority model, such as rating problems and issues, as follows:
    - Urgent and important.
    - Important but not urgent.
    - Urgent but not important.
    - Not important and not urgent.

Challenging Work Situation

- Purchasing local advertising for 30 percent less than corporate marketing could by buying off a local rate card and consulting a local agency. Navigating through the internal and political waters to accomplish this was quite challenging.

When Did You Make a Quick Decision?

- Hiring a sales manager during a first interview for a start-up operation.

When Did You Make the Wrong Decision?

- Had a panel interview a potential sales candidate. I was leaning against hiring the candidate, but the consensus was to hire him. We did, and he did not work out. (*The key here is to avoid citing a wrong decision that will scare the hiring manager away.*)

How Would You Develop a New Business Plan?

- Begin with a sales objective—the written outcome of what you hope to achieve.
- Analyze the market, competition, customer segments, the niche we fill, the distribution strategy, compensation, and supporting procedures. Break the business down into as small competencies as possible and work on those foundations.
- Develop metrics from which to measure success and determine opportunities for improvement.

How Do You Improve Low Morale?

- Recognize that morale is often a reflection of leadership.
- Talk "team," including support and corporate staff.
- Utilize team selling and team project planning.
- Alternate who leads sales and other meetings.
- Schedule team outings.
- Set up a sales "cup" trophy or something similar.
- Get staff exposed to senior management.
- Keep staff informed—more information to staff is better than less.
- Be sure that staff members believe I would fight for them to support their goals.
- Set a credible example.

What Is Your Coaching Philosophy?

- Coaching is important so that employees are self-sufficient.
- Build coaching based on balanced feedback.
- Ensure that employees believe I'm *for* their success.
- Discuss with employees what they do and did well and then mention an area of improvement and then an agreed-upon developmental action.
- Create a fun environment—you can't keep your foot on the gas all the time.
- Focus on strengths.
- "Pull" style—get team members to identify their weaknesses and corrective action.
- Don't overwhelm them with a lot of actions—do it in small doses.

How Do You Matrix-Manage?

- The issue is effectively managing multiple projects and activities simultaneously.
    - At a previous employer I simultaneously managed:
        - Direct sales in city 1.
        - Indirect sales in city 1.
        - Inside sales in city 1.
        - Direct sales in city 2.
        - Indirect sales in city 2.
        - Inside sales in city 2.
        - Marketing for both markets and cities.
- How?
    - Start with a plan for each project and/or channel and itemize needed activities.
    - Manage both end results and leading indicators before the end is reached. This prevents a surprise from happening on the back end.
    - Identify projected outcomes before they happen and make adjustments to the plan when necessary.
    - Stay organized: stay closely tied to your calendar and do not procrastinate. I use a Microsoft Outlook calendar. Never let your e-mail inbox build up. Read and file e-mails but get through them and schedule time when necessary.
    - Rank each task as A, B, or C. Make sure to get highest-priority tasks completed first.

Distinguish Between a Strategy and a Tactic

- A strategy is what you want to accomplish, a broad direction.
- A tactic is the specific road map, or steps, you take to get there.

How Do You Motivate Employees?

- Give personnel updates to my manager when he comes to visit my office. That way, when he sees the employees, he can reference something they did. The employee will know I moved his or her accomplishment up the management chain and feel recognized.

- Invite all employees to lunch when my manager visits from out of town.
- Always provide balanced feedback; focus on the "pluses" and reinforce them. When discussing employees' growth opportunities, I use phrases like "that isn't like you at all" to get their buy-in.
- Give the entire staff quarterly updates on the business, a state of the union, and then take them out for a barbeque or bowling—or both.
- Provide lots of updates to employees. As a rule, never insulate employees from information. They'll hear about things anyway. They'll trust you if they hear it from you. They'll feel more connected if they have information.
- Always have one-on-ones with employees.
- Specific examples:
  - Helped two employees get promoted when they deserved it. The people on my staff knew I would support their growth when the right opportunity popped up.
  - Sent a cookie garden to the marketing team members in another city to thank them for helping us with a task.
  - Provided shopping mall gift certificates to customer service reps for doing things well.
  - Created an out-of-process sales contest in which American Express gift checks were given for reaching sales targets.

If You Were Vice President of This Company, What Would You Do?

- Start with people. I would make sure the right team members are in the right roles, ensure tight performance management to help them become most successful, and emphasize high morale and culture.
- Focus on wider issues—longer-term as well as day-to-day issues.
- Gather information, establish objectives, and hold management more accountable.
- Ensure that plans are in place to reach sales goals. Make midlevel managers more accountable. Hire right.
- Be more visible to the entire team vertically to build morale and hear the line-level challenges.

How Do You Develop a Sales Strategy?

- Analyze the current situation.
- Understand competitive advantage.
- Decide where to focus resources.
- Identify, prioritize, and drive change.
- Continually monitor performance and review strategy.

Developing a Sales Strategy

Analyze	Plan	Implement
Market conditions	Define purpose	Prioritize change
Team	Set boundaries	Plan change
Products	Identify competitive advantages	Review operational targets
	Create budget	Motivate people to execute
		Hold reviews
		Change where necessary, modify tactics, assess

What Are Your Key Sales Management Skills?

- Developing the right salesperson profile.
- Recruiting the right people.
- Training.
- Coaching.
- Allocating territory assignments and customers.
- Monitoring activity levels.
- Monitoring closing ratios.
- Analyzing results.
- Recognizing and rewarding achievements.
- Dealing with failure.

I did end up getting an offer for this position. Did the hiring vice president ask me any of these questions? Maybe two or three, but no more. However, by completing this exercise, I was better prepared to interject these accomplishments and approaches to business than I would have been had I not written all this out.

It's like preparing a game plan for a big football game. You can watch all the videos you want of past games, but you never really know what plays they'll throw at you. But the more prep you do, the more those plays will look familiar, and the better you'll be able to turn a great defense into an offense.

PART 1

BEFORE THE INTERVIEW

Researching the Company

JOE PASCUAL IS a 36-year-old sales manager. He has worked in the telecommunications industry his entire 14-year career. He began as a sales representative, moved to marketing and then moved back to sales, became a general manager, and even started up new operations for one of the largest telecommunications companies in the world.

In 2014 Joe decided to look for a new position. He had rock-solid credentials, experience, and references. He began circulating his résumé and applied online and direct to a few companies that had posted director-level opportunities.

After three months of doing this, he had made no real progress. In the worst telecommunications market in recent history, he felt fortunate to have his current position. He did not have high expectations.

Then one night he was scanning Monster.com and saw a terrific opportunity. It was a position as regional director of sales for an industry leader. The job posting included the following job description:

> *This Regional Sales Director position will be responsible for launching and operating a profitable sales territory that satisfies [hiring company's] customer requirements & meets the territory's revenue objectives. You will manage five acquisition- & retention-focused sales branches selling local, long-distance, and Internet services to businesses. This position requires the candidate to have successful*

sales management experience, verifiable, and experience starting up new sales operations. This position will also be responsible for the selection, training, and development of a professional sales staff.

Joe posted his résumé for the position and received a screening interview with a human resources (HR) manager. The interviewer asked Joe many questions, and he did his best to answer them. He answered the questions based on his background and his accomplishments.

The interview was over, and Joe did not feel he had developed a strong rapport with the HR manager. Most candidates can tell if they are going on to the next round based on how the interview went—both from a good position fit and from the standpoint of how much rapport developed.

Joe never heard anything. After about five days, and not wanting too much more time to pass, he called the HR recruiter and asked for feedback. The recruiter was lukewarm and told Joe the company was still seeking other candidates.

To Joe's surprise, he received a second call for an interview with the hiring manager. He called us to prep him for his second interview, determined to do a better job this time.

After we reviewed the preparation he had done thus far, we found no apparent connection between his experience as depicted on his résumé and what the company was trying to hire. He did not *customize* his prepared answers to anticipated questions for this opportunity. He saw a great opportunity and did not think to spend extra time trying to understand what the hiring company was looking for and how he would enable those results.

Here is how we guided his interview preparation.

It's Really All About *Them*

To develop a solutions-based interview, you need to uncover and understand the needs of the hiring company. What are its hot-button, key business drivers that keep the company's executives up at night? Identify those and position yourself as a contributory solution, and that's when you've really scored.

Research the Company

Researching a company, as with anything else today, is much easier than it was even a decade ago. You can spend 90 minutes on the Internet and learn more than you could in a full day of doing research the old-fashioned way at the library.

Why Research?

The reasons you want to research the company are to:

- Understand how it stands financially (no finance background required for this). Is it profitable, free of investigations? How much cash does it have in the bank compared with its competitors? One sure sign of a company's health is the amount of debt it carries compared with that of its competitors in the industry.
- Identify the company's key partners, vendors (companies it buys from), and customers (companies it sells to). This is helpful when you are trying to network to get to key decision makers for referrals. Think of drawing out the six degrees of separation to find the shortest connection between you and the company (preferably the hiring manager).
- Understand the company's key products: which are the "cash cows" and are in place for the future?
- Understand the company nomenclature and terminology so that you "speak its speak" when you finally meet.
- Discover areas where the business might need you to help it.

Use this information if you decide to build a business plan for your interview. A sample is provided in Chapter 19. The research you do here will help determine the needs you uncover.

Great Research Tools

What follows is a list of tools that can be accessed through the Internet to learn more about a target company. Using the Internet is not mandatory, but the research you can do online is much more efficient than conducting paper research.

- *Company's website.* You must visit the company's website, which in all probability is something it does have. Review the company's products, news releases first and the rest second. This should give you a good grounding in its business operations and approach.
  - *Annual report.* The annual report for a company provides the mission statement, strategic direction, financial standing, and health. It will give you a snapshot of the company's products and organizational structure.
- *Google.com.* This one is obvious. When you get to the search screen, enter the company name, the name of the hiring manager, and anything else relevant, such as industry data.
- *LinkedIn.* You can get great information about who works there and whom you can connect with, and you can even see posts from team members to get some inside information.
- *Facebook.* With Facebook you can find out current product offers, promotions, and fun facts that will reflect more of the company spirit and culture than you may find on the company's website.
- *Twitter.* You'll get quick visibility to products, PR releases, and job postings on Twitter.
- *Hoovers.com. This is an online database of over 225 million business records.* Even without a subscription, terrific information can be gathered by searching the site.
- *Yahoo.com (finance), MSN.com (finance), and Quicken.com.* These are other good sites to search.

Now What?

Every time you research or learn something about the company, ask yourself, "So what?" You need to digest the information, interpret it at some level, and determine how you fit into what you're reading to enable the improvement of the business. Imagine you're researching to develop a 15-minute presentation on the company and the direction in which it is heading over the next 12 to 18 months. Or imagine your presentation is about how your discipline may *enable* the company to reach its overarching objectives.

Here are some sample *so-what?* questions you can ask yourself as you conduct your research:

- Who are the company's major strategic partners, vendors, and customers?
  - Whom do I know at these companies who can provide me with a referral, contact name, or reference to separate me from the pack?
- What are the company's major business units?
- What are the company's key business drivers, its key challenges, and areas of pain?
- Who are the major competitors?
- What has happened recently that is of interest (new hires, reorganizations, product launches)?

You = Value

Now that you've researched the company properly, you need to understand how you fit into the picture. In the following chapters we will discuss:

- What is happening on the other end: at the company.
- How to spin, or customize, your message to meet the needs of the company and the interviewer.
- What questions to ask the interviewer both to learn more and to gain credibility.

Why Do This at All?

At home you probably get hit with a lot of direct marketing in the form of junk mail, spam e-mail, and telemarketing calls. These contacts that companies make with you are not specific; they're the same calls they make to everyone else. How do you feel about that? Right. Now suppose a telemarketer called you and actually knew what your hot buttons were, understood your values, and was presenting something to make your life genuinely easier.

That's where we need to get you. Understanding the target company allows you to:

- Understand the company's business and communicate using its language. This will increase your credibility.
- Understand the ways the business needs help and position yourself as a value add by:
  - Helping it make (or save) money.
  - Helping it increase profitability.
  - Helping it increase the productivity of its assets.

Preinterview: Researching the Company

Remember Joe Pascual at the beginning of the chapter? Joe needed to conduct some research to prepare for his interview. He needed to learn to spin his responses in the direction of the company's needs.

We will begin the questioning section that follows with questions you should ask yourself about the company to get a grip on what it does and where it needs improvement. Convey the idea that you can enable that improvement in the interview, and you've really got something.

It's a good idea to conduct company research before the interview so that you can step up to the challenge and answer questions intelligently. At a minimum, know what a company's products and services are, why they interest you, and how you can help support them.

Determine which of the two types of companies your target company is: publicly traded on stock exchanges or privately held. Privately held companies are more difficult to find information about. They are not required to file documentation because there are no shareholders. Much information is limited to directories and local publications and some trade magazines. Sales figures are usually estimates.

TIPS >

Here are some tips to keep in mind when preparing to research a company:

- Publicly owned companies are usually easier to find information about than are privately owned ones.
- Corporations as a whole are generally easier to find information about than are their subsidiaries or divisions.
- Large, nationally known corporations are always easier to find information about than are local or regional ones.

Questions You Should Ask Yourself

- Where is the company based? Does it have a parent company? Does it have subsidiaries? Where are they located? Is the company international?
- What are the size of the company, the address, the phone number, a description of business, the ticker symbol if public, net sales, volume, and so on?
- What are the SIC or NAICS codes? These codes help classify and describe what industries and services the company provides and are becoming more widely used in directories and statistical sources (*this is a secondary research component*).
- What type of business is it? What are its products and brands?
- How big is the industry it's in? What are the predictions for the industry? Is it a growing industry, stagnant, or collapsing?
- Who are the company's competitors, and what do you know about them? How does the company compare with its competitors?

These questions, above and below, are designed to give you a foundation of information about the company. You should be able to apply common sense to the information you uncover regardless of your business acumen level. *Your objective is to learn about the company and make the connection of how you will fit into the picture and enable the company to be better.*

- Is the company ranked as a Fortune 500, Forbes 500, or Northwest 100 company?
- What events could affect the company? How is the company doing compared with the industry it is in?
- Is the company expanding, contracting, or stagnant?
- What are the company's sales, income, and indebtedness? What does this say about the company?
- What are the predictions for the company? What are analysts and news reports saying?
- What are its strengths and weaknesses?
- What do you know about its past? What mistakes has it made? What are some of its major events?
- What is the company's mission statement or philosophy? Does the company seem to be following it? What are its future plans?
- What do you know about those who run the company?
- How socially responsible is the company?

Company research involves finding out as much information as you can to determine if it is a place where you would like to work. Company research consists of reading the company's website, press kit, annual report, and other literature. You need to talk to people who have worked there. Find out what its competitors and clients say about the company.

Do research to determine if the company is really a place where you want to work. Be sure that the company's mission and values match yours. Also, find out about the corporate culture:

- Are interactions between employees formal or informal?
- What is the dress code?
- How does the company approach human rights issues?
- What are its standards?

Seek out information that will help you determine your fit in the organization, possibilities for advancement, and company stability.

Here are some more questions you may want answered before you apply for a job:

1. What qualities does the company seek in an employee? For example, does it look for creativity, initiative, perseverance, accuracy, and punctuality?
2. What kind of atmosphere does the company have? For example, is it tense or relaxed, formal or informal, dynamic or static?
3. What are the company's hiring procedures and policies? For example, does it hire frequently? Does it hire only through referrals?
4. What developments or changes is the company planning? This information can help you identify a growing need in the company and company stability. For example, if the company is planning to develop online business services, it will need people with Internet skills.

If you complete even half this research, you will be more prepared than will most of the other candidates. Few candidates conduct this much research, and fewer have the business acumen to interpret what the information is telling them and how they fit into the current business situation. Conducting this research will allow you to connect your skills to the hiring company's needs.

Identifying Company Culture

IN NEARLY EVERY interview I've been on, the interviewer has asked me what I know and think about his or her company's culture. And every time I interview a candidate, I ask that question. In 2014 I interviewed a candidate for a district manager position leading a group of retail stores. The employer was a company that greatly valued culture; it represented itself as a faith-based company, much like Chick-fil-A and Hobby Lobby.

Michael: *"So tell me what you know about our company and what you think about our culture."*

Candidate: *"Well, I know you guys are into God. I think that's cool; I've been hearing a lot about God lately, and it's cool you all are into that."*

You just can't make this stuff up. With all the information out on the Internet about the hiring company, that was that one thing he took away about the company. This is an extreme answer, and one I'll cherish the rest of my career. But how should you actually respond to this question? How do you identify the culture?

What Is Company Culture?

First, there are two types of cultures to be aware of: company culture and manager's culture. The latter is more prevalent. A strong manager, effective at cultivating culture or not, will overshadow the company culture. If you report to a poor manager in a great company, you'll be miserable. If you report to a great cultural leader in a company with no real culture identified, it could be a great experience. Identifying the company culture is fairly easy to do, and you'd only do two things here. One is identifying the actual culture and talking about it. Second, even if your research is a little inaccurate, you're still messaging to the interviewer you've done your homework, which is really the objective.

Culture is a company's value system, how that company treats its team members (good keyword), vendors, and customers and handles employee development. You can see examples of culture in what companies say in public release statements, in how they have handled reduction in staff, and in how they manage work-life balance for team members.

In late 2006, Radio Shack was undergoing a large reduction in workforce. Here is how it communicated which team members would be laid off. All the employees were to be sitting at their computer at 8:45 a.m., and they would receive an e-mail saying whether they would be retained or released. If released, those team members were to go to a designated room to get their release package from human resources and then leave. Imagine the stress leading up to that within the entire organization! This is by no means representative of Radio Shack's entire culture: the then CEO thought it'd be a quick way to perform an unpleasant task. But it is indicative of the types of things you should look out for in a company's culture.

Corporate culture can be bucketed into a few types:

- *Hierarchy based.* Most commonly seen, this environment views management as organization leaders, leans on management to make decisions, and is less apt to open the strategic contribution to all team members not part of a leadership team.
- *Internally focused.* Not commonly seen, this kind of culture focuses on management and team members and is often driven by human resources. It can produce a great place to work, but it can also create a sluggish slow-to-market and response-to-customers environment.

- *Entrepreneurial focused.* This is certainly an environment that most nimble and successful corporations, like Google and Zappos, adhere to. As large as Southwest Airlines is, it prides itself on being creative and having an entrepreneurial spirit. And according to Tech Crunch, Ernst & Young internally initiated something called "The Innovation Challenge," where team members are encouraged to create new products and services. PricewaterhouseCoopers started something called the "PwC PowerPitch," where team members are encouraged to create new innovative initiatives, and if the company uses them, the creating team is awarded a significant reward.
- *Customer based.* This culture puts customers and the customer experience first. Productivity, good customer satisfaction scores, and performance management are priorities.

How to Identify Company Culture

1. Do some online research. If you're interviewing with Whole Foods or The Container Store, you will quickly see that those companies value culture and are very intentional about defining it and practicing it. Study third-party articles and the company website for anything documented on it. Most companies are neutral to identifying their culture, so you may have to decipher some of that yourself. On most large company websites, you will see a section on why you would want to work there.
2. Ask the person who is conducting that first interview with you to define the culture and his or her experience. Do that quickly so you can get some grounding for the rest of the interview.
3. Ask current team members.
4. Look at the dress code of the team members and check out the office decor. In 1997, I was interviewing with Sprint, and draped all around the walls were posters of The Rolling Stones (Sprint was sponsoring their tour). It struck me as a creative and fun culture. I ended up joining Sprint and began my 10-year run working there.

5. Pay attention to other team member vibes. Do the people seem happy to work there?

6. Ask the interviewer how the company handles the busiest season. How often are team member reviews conducted, and is the company disciplined about it? How often is training available, and what are examples of that?

What Is Your Culture?

You'll be asked by most interviewers how to define your culture. You should have a thoughtful answer to this. You're balancing two things: specifying what you want your ideal culture to be and making sure you do not overwhelm the interviewer by imposing your idea of a perfect work culture on him or her.

In the books *Firms of Endearment* by Rajendra S. Sisodia, David Wolfe, and Jagdish Sheth and *Conscious Capitalism* by John Mackey and Rajendra S. Sisodia, a half dozen-plus companies are profiled as championing a higher purpose for their organizations. These companies include Whole Foods, The Container Store, Costco, Southwest Airlines, Patagonia, and Google, among others. These companies focus on creating a work-life balance and a business that strives for their team members, customers, vendors, and community. They also promote a fun and creative environment. Do some research and pick apart the elements you relate to best and can speak to with some conviction.

Michael's Work Culture

As an example, let's delve into how I communicate my culture and values to coworkers and potential employees, how I would lead a prospective organization, and how would I define my group's past cultures.

When people enjoy what they do and their environment, they perform better. How do I create that kind of environment? By building a playful environment that encourages open communication and contribution. In the past we have scheduled monthly or bimonthly team-building events, such as a two-hour escape on a Friday to a local park to play bocce ball. In this event, the losers had to sing "You Are the Champions," played off of Queen's hit. This kind of seemingly silly event creates a relaxed environment and a great culture. You can't keep your foot on the gas all the time; if you performance-manage tightly without a release, the pressure will break the team.

Figure 2-1 depicts a chart inspired by my favorite management book, *The Cycle of Leadership* by Noel Tichy. It's a great book; pick it up. I once took the chart into an interview and talked about how team members need to be well equipped, taught patiently, and instructed on how to excel. You can't be autocratic and expect great results. That goes for management or parenting. The manager needs to be a tireless teacher who invests in the team so the team can fairly be accountable for results.

Another example in generating work culture is communicating the idea of always putting customers first, enterprise second. By putting customers—the group that actually provides the fuel to keep the

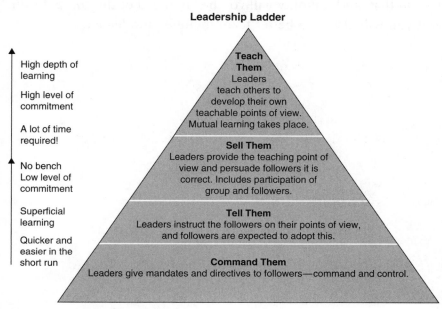

Figure 2-1 Cycle of leadership

company going—first, you get a pass on having people think you are promoting any personal agendas versus having your motives be perceived as selfish in nature.

Putting It Together

More than anything, be prepared. Very few candidates are well prepared for recognizing or communicating a company's culture. Do the research to identify your potential employer's culture, and be prepared to share your own.

1. Prior to the interview, write down around half a page of bullet points about the target company culture so that you have it handy. It is important to write them down instead of trying to memorize them. You are more likely to remember key points when you put them on paper.
2. Write out another half page about what your ideal company culture is, what your ideal group culture is, and how you make that happen.

Do that, and not only will you be far ahead of the competition, but you will also be a better team member and leader.

Social Media and the Job Search

Tom Kimmons is a sales director in Atlanta. For the last 5 years of his 20-year career, he has had a specialty in construction materials. Prior to that, he worked in the auto industry and power sports. Since he's been in materials the last five years or so, he got "branded" in that industry and had a difficult time getting interest from other industries. His job search lasted about seven months, and an interviewer (who did not hire him) suggested he amp up his profile on LinkedIn using an abbreviated résumé rich in keywords (keywords are explained later in this chapter). Within six weeks, an employer contacted him for an opportunity that fit his background, at a VP level. He ended up getting that position with his highest career compensation to date.

Social media sites such as LinkedIn, Facebook, and Twitter are awesome tools that have really come into their own of late. Two reasons mostly: (1) they're great tools for higher-quality and sometimes passive candidates, and (2) they're great tools to leverage your network and get your foot in the door.

LinkedIn

LinkedIn is the most active vehicle for job searching among the networking media sites. It's probably a runaway compared with the more social media sites such as Facebook, Twitter, and Instagram.

It's still not close to job boards like CareerBuilder and Monster as an opportunity source, but securing an interview using LinkedIn is big enough to be a staple for your resources, particularly if you're a white-collar professional. It's the biggest professional search engine.

Building Your Profile

Your Photo

LinkedIn members are connecting with people, not a blank box; therefore you'll need a picture for your profile. Some things you'll see occasionally, not often, are clip art–type images in your picture area, pictures that are slanted sideways, or photos that have poor image quality (blurry or grainy). One connection put his child in his profile photo, as if it were Facebook. Sometimes you'll see the casually dressed, goofy smile picture or the picture taken at a club with drink in hand.

You must remember that this is a professional tool and that potential employers will be viewing this page. Your picture should be an upper-body close-up of you in business or business casual attire, or it could be a head shot. The photo should be well lit and bright and should be professionally flattering. Not glamorous flattering, but pleasant. Your picture is really to help personalize your profile. A bad picture is worse than no picture.

Figure 3-1 is an example of a very nice picture of this LinkedIn member, but the wrong picture for this medium. It would be a great picture to share with friends or on Facebook, but not LinkedIn.

Look how much more credible and professional the picture of the same person is in Figure 3-2. Well framed, clear, a real professional profile picture.

Your Headline

Make it easy for the reader to know who you are and what you do by using a great descriptive headline. Examples include "Digital Marketing Manager," "Retail Store Manager," and "Supply Chain Management Director." This is the most important copy in your profile. The reason is that you only get so much of the reader's time,

Figure 3-1 "Before" picture

and if the title does not appear to be a fit, the rest may not get read. The same concept applies to your résumé too. The objective section of your résumé should fit the job description; otherwise a potential employer might pass on to the next résumé in the pile.

- Use an actual title like "Brand Marketing Manager" versus "Experienced Marketing Manager"; the former lends itself to more currency and credibility.
- If you're between jobs, make sure that you select "Accepting Messages" in the Open Link section and that you click on the Job Seeker option (Premium Account feature only), and don't put down "consultant" as your current gig unless you can substantiate it.

Figure 3-2 "After" picture

Your Summary

Write an interesting summary. Make it tight, easy to read, no typos! Generally, think like your résumé. A difference here is you get more creative writing freedom than with your résumé. Once you get rolling, look at some other profiles for inspiration. Particularly, look at the profiles of those who are more actively plugged into LinkedIn. The more active someone is, the more likely the person's profile is a good example.

Look at the two summaries shown in Figures 3-3 and 3-4, "before" and "after." The first has a typo (no space between "4" and "years,") and it has a bunch of buzzwords but no real description of what the person really does. Then look at the after. It's brief and explanatory and is lightly written to engage the reader.

Note about keywords. A keyword is a word or phrase used when someone conducts a search. The more keywords associated with your profile, the better for searchability. However, you want to make them free of empty calories. Words that come up in keyword searches include technical job terms, like *paralegal, performance management, point of sale, remote server, SEO.* Empty words that are not keywords include *dynamic, results oriented, team player*—you get the idea. These appear much more often than you'd think.

Make your summary short—no one will have an attention span to read a long paragraph in your profile. Keep each paragraph limited to four to five lines.

Figure 3-3 "Before" summary

Summary

Own and lead culture for $1.5B retail and wholesale company in Dallas. We define purpose and constantly refine culture initiatives because team members that are happy perform better and serve customers better. They also stay here longer so we get less turnover than most companies!

Figure 3-4 "After" summary

Your Experience

Just as you did for the summary, make this section tight and easy to read and be sure there are no typos. Compare the "before" and "after" experiences shown in Figures 3-5 and 3-6.

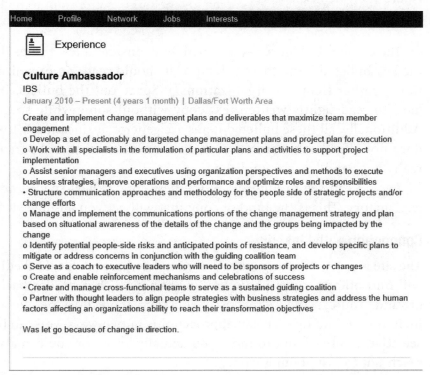

Figure 3-5 "Before" experience

Culture Ambassador
IBS
January 2010 – Present (4 years 1 month) | Dallas/Fort Worth Area

IBS is a privately held $1.5B company with over 1,000 team members based in Dallas. IBS is consistently rated at the top of the Dallas Best Places to Work surveys.

• Own culture initiatives within IBS

• Defining corporate purpose for the enterprise. Attended Conscious Capitalism workshop led by executives at Whole Foods, The Container Store, Patagonia, Zappos,and many others. Personally visited many of these companies to share culture initiatives and develop new ones
o Lead group of twelve representatives from each division/department within IBS on culture initiatives including annual team member offsite gathering with awards, presentations

• Own culture, morale and productivity surveys within each division and department. Based on those results, partner with the vice president of each to develop actionable plan of improvement. A couple of those included eliminating culture drains by creating accountability campaign, and another was coaching leaders in how to give monthly performance updates in a positive motivating approach

• Taught four two-day classes on how to coach managers on providing constructive criticism. These classes were intensive on role plays and received terrific feedback from all attendees. Later surveys with team members validated improved morale and performance based on improved interpersonal skills by the managers

Figure 3-6 "After" experience

The content in Figure 3-5 isn't bad, but consider a few things. In the last bulleted item, there is a typo (it should read "an organization's" rather than "an organizations"). Space out the bullets. It's hard to read tightly written text copy without some white space. Additionally, all these bulleted items are generic business copy that does not effortlessly communicate to the reader what this person really does and has accomplished.

As you can see in Figure 3-6, the new copy is well spaced and explanatory. This is the kind of copy that will get you an interview.

Connecting with LinkedIn

The site is pretty amazing; once you complete your profile, LinkedIn will find other people whom you may know with a similar background. You can then effortlessly click and send those people an invitation to link up. You can approach this in two ways: you can be selective and reach out to those you actually know, or you can also reach out to just about anyone.

Our recommendation is to connect only to those you know first. It can be distracting, even bothersome, to receive LinkedIn requests from people you do not know. And that can hurt more than no connection. If you do reach out to people you do not know, explain why you'd like to connect in your request to them.

The generic LinkedIn invitation request reads "I'd like to add you to my professional network." That standard copy is okay for your very close circle; your close friends and colleagues aren't going to think twice about getting that standard invitation copy. It's in requests to the people you do not know that you will need to add some personal copy.

Suppose you are reaching out to someone at Bank of America whom you do not know but who knows someone you know fairly well. That invite could look something like:

> Hi Maria, my name is Susan Parker, and we both know Paul Taylor. I work for Comerica now, and I'd like to learn more about Bank of America and talk to you later this month. Thanks! Really appreciate your help. —Susan

You don't have to request to talk to the person soon, but it is good to be transparent in your agenda and your message.

What to Avoid

With LinkedIn and the ease of connecting it offers, it's very possible to make casual mistakes that can impede your ultimate goal. Great attention to detail is necessary. So is following the street-smart tips listed below.

- Don't overdo it with your requests to connect with people you don't know—connect only if you have reason to! Put yourself in their shoes: you're established in your career, you have your solid network, and all of a sudden you get bombarded with inquiries to link up with people you do not know. It can be uncomfortable. When reaching out to someone you do not know, make sure to personalize a few lines of why you are reaching out. Use common sense: if you can't think of a good few personalized lines for your request, then you shouldn't send a request.
- Avoid "stalking" other people's profiles. Unlike on Facebook, LinkedIn shows you who has viewed your profile, which can be awkward if you visit someone's profile repeatedly.

- Posting comments, whether on your own or on people's LinkedIn posts, is great, but avoid posting any transparent sales pitches. It's the quickest way to turn your network off.
- Don't post personal, nonprofessional information, such as what your current relationship status is or where you'll be partying next weekend. Remember that this social media venue is very different from Facebook and Twitter—don't post anything you wouldn't want your boss to see!
- When you change your title, even if it's just a tweak, you will trigger LinkedIn to send a broadcast message to all in your network with a "congratulations on your new job" announcement. Avoid this! It can hurt your messaging because the people in your network and prospective employers will think you just got a new position. Go to "Privacy Settings" and turn off activity broadcasts.

Searching for Job Candidates Using LinkedIn

Employers are using LinkedIn more and more nowadays to find job candidates, especially for white-collar and more professional jobs. Why? They get a window into a candidate's skills and network. They can easily search and find candidates based on keywords, which yields high-quality contacts. In fact, some recruiters use LinkedIn as their primary candidate research tool.

LinkedIn claims that employees from all Fortune 500 companies are represented on LinkedIn. That's surely true. Sometimes recruiters will specifically want a candidate from a certain company or industry because of the person's training or performance standards.

Once while working for Sprint, I was recruiting for district sales managers and specifically sought them out from Estee Lauder, knowing how strong the company was in training, customer engagement, and retail selling. I typed in the keywords "district manager" and "Estee Lauder" in the search box at the top of LinkedIn's main page and found some great candidates to reach out to. LinkedIn provides a very efficient way to search and penetrate specific companies and industries, and Fortune 500 companies use it for that very reason.

A referred candidate is a lower risk to a company than a non-referred one, and often internal recruiters will ask their employees to post an opening on their LinkedIn profiles to spark up a good candidate pool.

Job Searching with LinkedIn

There are three primary ways to use LinkedIn to secure interviews:

1. Use the "Jobs" tab to find job postings in your area. You will often see positions posted here that are not on Monster.com or CareerBuilder.com, so it's a worthy complement. Applying is very easy—in fact, it is easier than on some other sites.
2. Uncover job opportunities on other sites, like Monster.com, and then search for the company on LinkedIn to connect with company employees, to learn more about the company, and to get in the door.
3. You could also identify companies themselves, instead of looking for a specific job opportunity, and research them. Browse through their employees and request a connection if any of them share a network connection with you. Be specific on why and make advice your angle for reaching out.

For some great examples of how to use LinkedIn and other social media, check out *How to Find a Job on LinkedIn, Facebook, Twitter, Google+* by Brad Schepp and Debra Schepp.

Google+

Up until early 2013, I was not very familiar with Google+ or Google Docs. One night my then 13-year-old son was working on a project that was shared with a group of four. He was collaborating with his classmates in real time on Google Docs. The information was saved constantly, and the site allowed contributions from other team members to be tracked—it was pretty amazing. When I was writing my first book in 1994, I'd written about 10 pages of a chapter when my computer locked up; I had to restart it, lost my work, spent a couple hours on the ledge . . . and from then on saved my work constantly in two places. Where were easy back-up options back then?!

On to Google+, a separate tool from Google Docs. Why Google+? With more popular social sites like Facebook, LinkedIn, Twitter, and Instagram, why bother with a medium that is less socially known? One big reason is all your content and posts are connected to Google's search engine. Another reason is the ease of separating "circles" of your personal and professional (and other) connections. As of this writing, Google+ is a much less applicable tool for job searching, specifically compared with LinkedIn. But it does offer advantages that are more social in orientation than LinkedIn (though less so than Facebook). And hey, you're looking to open up as many opportunities as you can, so what can this hurt? Setting up your profile will take all of a half hour, considering you just wrote some awesome content for your LinkedIn profile that you can leverage. Of course, do this after you've done a thorough job on LinkedIn.

TIPS

Here are some ideas to get you going on Google+:

- Create your profile and make sure it is more professional than social. If you're using it for job searching, apply the same principles as you did for your LinkedIn profile. You should be able to leverage that content too.
- When you get into it, separate your circles into professional ones and personal ones.
- As you did for LinkedIn, seek out a network. One cool thing about Google+ compared with LinkedIn (and why it's more like Twitter) is that you can follow people who you want and group them how you want without disclosure, even if they do not reciprocate.
- You can use your Google+ profile as a link to your other resources or profiles (Twitter, Facebook, LinkedIn, your own web page, etc.).
- You can post some additional pictures of your work to strengthen your profile.

Twitter and Facebook

These two social media staples are so well known. Hundreds of millions of people subscribe to Facebook and Twitter. There are some different schools of thought on using Facebook and Twitter actively (posting) for your job search. Our personal opinion is that LinkedIn and Google+ will provide you with enough of a professional online presence, and using Facebook and Twitter for active postings more may be redundant and risky. Using Facebook and Twitter as professional resources in addition to LinkedIn is up to your own preference.

By all means, you can create Twitter and Facebook accounts to follow all target employers and groups. By doing this, you'd be able to benefit from a larger pool of information on specific company news and job opportunities. Just be supersensitive to what you push out on your profiles for all to see.

Here's why. LinkedIn is considered the leading professional networking tool, but Twitter and Facebook are much more social. With a more social environment comes less professionalism and a lower guard. That's okay if you're an athlete under contract, a media person, an entertainer—your posts are low risk. It's combining the social part with the professional part that could get tricky. If you're seeking a new job, you need to project a tight, professional image. For most people—though definitely not all—switching back and forth between media is hard to do.

With Twitter, it is hard to not post random, meaningless but fun tweets. Same with Facebook. There's just not a place for that in the job search. You can build your brand by posting informative tweets, but for most positions, this will not be a huge value add. If you're in marketing or advertising or some healthcare industries, for example, you may be able to create a more social feel to your posts. For most other industries, these types of posts won't work.

TIPS

Here are some things to keep in mind if you use Twitter or Facebook:

- The number one social media site where employers can determine the character and personality of potential job candidates is Facebook. Be sure you clean up and professionalize your Facebook page, or be sure to adjust your privacy settings so that nonprofessional material is not visible to anyone outside your friends list. Make sure to follow companies and people you like for industry and company information.
- Follow the company's job portal Twitter account in addition to the main company account. This will allow you to scope out any tweets about job opportunities in the company.
- Do not tweet personal or unprofessional messages. Be aware that your tweets are one of the things that will pop up when potential employers search you—and they will search. Whether you use Twitter and Facebook socially or for a job search, you should be mindful of typos, foul language, and other inappropriate content.
- Use a similar profile to what you use in LinkedIn—something like your LinkedIn headline and summary.
- Provide a link to your résumé and LinkedIn page.

Securing the Interview

THERE ARE SEVERAL primary sources for job leads:

- Job boards (Monster.com, Careerbuilder.com, etc.)
- Social networking (for example, LinkedIn)
- Personal networking
- Contact with companies directly
- Executive recruiters and employment agencies

Other sources include trade journals, job fairs, college placement offices, and state employment offices. One of the most difficult tasks in life is securing work and planning a career. A career is important to everyone, and so you must create a plan of action by utilizing more than one career design strategy.

Networking

Without question, the most common way people find out about and obtain new positions is through networking. Networking is *people connecting*, and when you connect with people, you begin to assemble your network. Once that network is in place, you will make new contacts and communicate with established members. People in your network will provide advice, information, and support in helping you achieve your career goals and aspirations.

Networking accounts for up to 70 percent of the new opportunities uncovered. So what is networking? Many people assume they should call all the people they know personally and professionally and ask if those people know any companies that are hiring. A successful networker's approach is different.

A successful networker starts by listing as many names as possible on a sheet of paper. These names can include family members, relatives, friends, coworkers and managers (past and present), other industry contacts, and anyone else you know. The next step is to formulate a networking presentation. Keep in mind that it need not address potential openings. In networking, the aim is to call your contacts and ask for career or industry advice. The point is, you're positioning yourself not as a desperate job hunter but as a researcher. It is unrealistic to think that you will go far by asking people for advice like this:

> *Mark, thanks for taking some time to talk with me. My company is likely to lay people off next month, and I was wondering if your company had any openings or if you know of any.*

This person hasn't said what he does, has experience in, or wants to do. Mark is likely to respond with "No, but I'll keep you in mind should I hear of anything." What do you think the odds are that Mark will contact this person again?

A better approach is to ask for personal or industry advice and to work on developing the networking web:

> *Mark, Paul Jonathan at CNA suggested I give you a call. He and I have worked together for some time, and he mentioned that you work in finance and are the controller of Allied Sensors. I work in cost accounting and feel you'd likely be able to offer some good career advice. I'd really appreciate some time. Could we get together for lunch sometime in the next week or so?*

You have now asked for advice, not for a job. People are much more willing to help someone who has made them feel good about themselves or who appears genuinely to appreciate their help. This strategy can be approached in many ways. You can ask for job search advice (including résumé or cover letter advice); overall career advice (as shown previously); industry advice; key contacts; information about various companies, people, and industries; and other people they know.

It is important that the person you network through like you. When someone gives you a reference, it is a reflection of that person. People will not put themselves at personal or professional risk if they aren't confident that you will reflect well on them. Finally, send each person you speak with a thank-you letter or e-mail. That courtesy will be remembered for future contacts.

Six Degrees of Separation

In addition to traditional networking for opportunities, there is another very effective way to leverage networking in today's economy. Suppose you go to Monster.com and uncover a great opportunity with Cisco Systems, Bristol-Myers Squibb, or a new company. Before blindly sending in your résumé and a brief cover letter to that company (or recruiter), immediately ask around and try to find a reference you can leverage to get to the hiring manager. Follow the rules of "six degrees of separation"; there is a good chance you can get a personal introduction to that person.

The idea behind the six degrees of separation is that you may be no more than six (two or three in a large organization) people or degrees from networking to get connected with an employee at the company you are targeting. See Figure 4-1. When you take advantage of this strategy, you have engineered a reference and have networked through the back door.

Another terrific strategy is to have your best references send in letters of recommendation to the hiring manager during the interview process. The determination you demonstrate by developing these references from your network will be perceived as the kind of determination you will demonstrate on the job. Companies desperately need good employees. Sell yourself as one, and most companies will find a place for you.

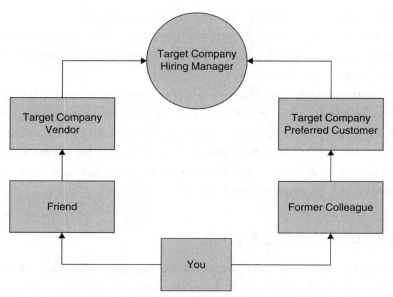

Figure 4-1 Six degrees of separation

A Dallas client of ours, John, was looking for a position with T-Mobile. The company website had a posting for a position it wanted to fill in Atlanta. But how do you avoid being batched in the plethora of résumés these companies receive for each posting, especially in today's economy? Here is what we did: we worked with the candidate to see if he knew anyone at T-Mobile. After a few days of asking around, it turned out that John's girlfriend's friend in Chicago works there. So we called her and got the name of her VP.

John called him in Seattle, and he actually picked up the phone, in part because John called before hours, when things were slow, and he waited until the VP answered the phone, not leaving a voice mail. John gave the VP a quick "elevator pitch" of his background and what his goals were, and the VP referred him to that region's VP. John then reached that VP and by that point had a few names to drop, positioning himself as a referred candidate.

The new VP had John get in touch with an HR recruiter in Kansas City, and a few weeks later John secured an interview and a position.

The whole networking exercise took just two days but enabled John to scoop hundreds of other candidates. You too should think of creative ways to network "internally."

Contacting Companies Directly

Aren't there one or two companies you've always wanted to work for? Ideally you know someone who will introduce you to key contacts there or inform you of future openings. The best way to get introduced to a targeted company is to have a current employee personally introduce you or make an introductory phone call for you. You could make the introduction and reference the employee you know. We'll get into this later, but if you don't know anyone at a targeted company, a recruiter may be a good source of contact, even if it involves no job order for him or her. LinkedIn is a great way to search for team members there and discover how you may be connected with them.

You could send an unsolicited résumé, but the likelihood of this panning out is low. Most large-profile companies receive thousands of résumés a year, and few are acted on. Mass-mailed résumés are rarely an effective approach. Part of the problem is that too many résumés are written as past job descriptions *and are not customized toward a targeted position.*

Conrad Lee, a retained Boca Raton recruiter, believes that "information is the most important thing in contacting companies directly. Don't call just one person in the company and feel that is sufficient. That person may have their own job insecurities or be on a performance improvement plan. You should contact 5 to 10 people and only then can you say you contacted that company directly." New job search strategies all entail targeting a select few smaller companies (under 750 employees, as larger companies are still downsizing) intensely rather than blanketing a thousand generically.

Contacting the head of your functional specialty in that company is a good start. Is it hard? Yes. You're facing rejection, probably feeling that you're bothering busy people or begging or maybe even feeling that you're inferior. Would you feel inferior if you were calling hotels and ticket agencies for Super Bowl information? Of course not. What if someone can't help you? You just get back on the phone until you achieve your goal. These contacts should be approached the same way. You have a great product to sell—yourself. Position yourself as someone of value and as a product that can contribute to the target company.

The key is to position yourself for individual situations. This requires specialized letters, résumés, and strategies tailored for each situation.

One trick is to call the company you are targeting and try to get the name of the person in charge of the department where you would like to work. If you don't know, call the receptionist and ask her or him who that is and perhaps who a vendor or two might be (such as an accounting firm or ad agency). Finally, check the company website for the latest news. Now you have something interesting to talk about when you reach the hiring manager.

Increase Your Odds—*Get In*

There are two different things you need to do to increase your odds when you contact companies directly. The first is to network your way internally to the decision maker. The second is to get an internal reference.

With small companies this can be difficult, but that is not the case with large Fortune 1000 companies. If you circulate and network effectively, you should be no more than two or three degrees from any major company, particularly if you're grounded in that industry.

Create a "family tree" of relationships you have with others and map out each one by industry. Start asking around for people who work for your targeted company or an affiliate (key customer, strategic partner, vendor) of that company. Keep looking. If you come up empty, go to a local restaurant for lunch or a happy hour spot that is near the company's office. Be subtle and ask around. You will find someone. Strike up a neutral conversation and then offer to treat that person to lunch in return for some information.

If these people like you, in almost all cases they will refer you internally. You've scored. An internal reference is worth more than any other kind.

Classified Advertising

When you depend on classified advertisements to locate job openings, you limit yourself to only 7 to 10 percent or less of available jobs, plus you are competing with thousands of job hunters who are reading the same ads. Keep in mind that the majority of these ads are for lower-wage positions. Do not disregard the classifieds but don't limit your options by relying too heavily on them. Answering ads is more effective at lower levels than at higher ones.

If you use this method, an entry-level position or an administrative support position is more likely to be found than a director's position, but it is easy to review advertisements. Check the local paper on Sunday, the paper of the largest metropolitan area near where you live, and even a few national papers such as the *Wall Street Journal* (or its advertisement summary, the *National Business Employment Weekly*) and the *New York Times*.

You may gain insight by looking at ads that don't necessarily match your background. You may see an ad that says "Due to our expansion in the Northeast we are looking for . . ." You have just learned of an expanding company that may need you. Review papers that have good display ads, such as the *Los Angeles Times*, the *Chicago Tribune*, and any other major Sunday edition.

Here is an interesting tactical suggestion. Once you've identified a job you are interested in, *call* the company. Many classified ads list a fax number but no company name or main number. They encourage you to fax your résumé but not to call. In most companies a fax number is a derivative extension of the main number. If the fax number is NXX-5479, there is a good chance that the main number is NXX-5000 or NXX-5400. With that number you can call and hunt for information, write the company a more interesting and industry-specific letter, and position yourself ahead of the people who didn't use this method.

Then, when you respond to the ad, write about the company rather than just saying, "I am answering your ad." Package the résumé and cover letter in a U.S. Priority Mail envelope so that it stands out, and you will be guaranteed to at least be reviewed, which is your first objective.

Executive Recruiters and Employment Agencies

Without some knowledge of the recruiting industry, choosing an appropriate recruiter can be as difficult as choosing an employee. There are over 6,000 recruiters of some kind in the United States. Some are large chains such as Robert Half Inc., and some are private recruiters that are more like consultants. Here is a brief overview of the recruiting industry as it relates to conducting your job search and developing your résumé.

Types of Recruiting Agencies

Executive recruiters fall into two major categories: contingency employment agencies and retained search firms. Traditionally, contingency agencies focus on the lower end of the hiring segment, from entry level through middle management. Retained search firms specialize in senior-level professionals and executives. The two types are different in the ways they recruit and charge for their services.

Contingency Recruiting Agencies

Contingency agencies, like management recruiters, charge a fee to the employer only when the candidate is hired. The contingency recruiter generally will perform some prescreening for the employer and then send a pool of candidates to the employer for the company to screen and interview. Rates usually range from 20 to 30 percent of the employee's first year's salary. The salary level of a position that a contingency firm is filling may range from $40,000 to $150,000.

Retained Search Firms

Retained search firms are hired by a company for a period of time. They are paid as a consultant whether they fill a search or not.

The employers pay retained search firms, as they do a contingency search firm. However, retained firms act more like an employee of the company, as many consultants do. They are less receptive to a candidate approaching them than a contingency recruiter is. Still, this is a channel worth pursuing.

One reason firms are retained and paid is that they are searching for hard-to-fill positions, which takes time and money. There is no guarantee they will find appropriate candidates, so they need some working capital to carry them through. A retained recruiter might get about a third of the employee's first year's salary. The salary range of a position this recruiter might fill may vary between $100,000 and the millions that a senior-level executive might earn.

TIPS > **Dos and Don'ts**

- Don't ever sign an exclusive with a recruiter.
- Don't pay a recruiter—that should come from the employer.
- Do focus on recruiters who specialize in your industry (healthcare, etc.), discipline (accounting, etc.), or geographic area.
- Do try to get a referral to a recruiter. This will help you find a good one and help you gain more credibility with the recruiter; it also will get the recruiter to become your advocate.
- Do make friends with some headhunters while you are employed so that they know you when you're hottest—employed and most marketable.

Online Services and Job Boards

Online technology has changed the way job seekers locate employment opportunities. Job hunters are now connecting with hiring authorities electronically. Thousands of astute individuals have tapped into these powerful new technologies (databases, electronic bulletin boards on the Internet, and other online employment services) to achieve their career goals.

There are many books dedicated to this subject. And many independent websites are dedicated to job postings. You may also look at your targeted employer's page; employers almost always list job postings that fall below an executive level. Still, the best methods of contact are still personal, because many positions are not posted, and, when they are, the poster may be flooded with responses.

When you are on the web, do several different searches for both keywords and the industry or discipline that is your specialty. Also, contact the local newspaper for additional online sources specific to your metropolitan area.

The top sites that house these opportunities include:

- Monster.com
- Careerbuilder.com
- LinkedIn.com

TIPS

Although there are many great resources to help you in an online search, here are a few tips to keep in mind:

1. Have a good idea of what types of jobs you are seeking. That will make the search on these online sites more narrow in scope and productive. Have geography and keywords prepared in advance. These two objectives should be completed anyway as part of developing your résumé.

2. Have two résumés at hand: a "finished" Microsoft Word document to send as an attachment and a nonformatted text-only résumé to copy and paste into an e-mail. The content should be the same. There will be times when you may post only plain text into some companies' recruiting websites, as well as times when you need to copy and paste your résumé into the body of an e-mail. Plan to post your résumé at these sites, as well as sending it directly to recruiters and employers.

3. Take the time to understand how the sites work before jumping in headfirst.

4. Print out copies of everything you see that is of interest on a site. It will help you for future reference. Also, catalog the companies that you send e-mails and résumés to so that you won't send redundant "applications."

5. Provide a personal e-mail address, not the one of your current employer. Check your e-mail daily, as that is often where you will receive the first reply.

6. Make sure your résumé is very specific about your experience and what you want to do. The folks reading these résumés are doing so online and will not give a lot of time to each; make it easy for them to get to your qualifications and objectives quickly and effortlessly. A concise summary is critical. Our book *202 Great Resumes* offers numerous examples of targeted résumés with excellent summary sections.

Behind the Scenes: Into the Interviewer's Mind

WHEN YOU ATTEND an interview, the hiring manager and HR manager hope to hire you. The easiest thing for them to do is move beyond the hiring process and get back to work. Hiring is costly and tiresome for a company, which is a consensus among many of the hiring managers and HR managers with whom we've worked. Hiring managers are hoping to see a candidate take the position, to rise up and show them he or she wants it and is the right fit. Their work is most difficult when there is no clear choice of a candidate and they have to work through all the candidates.

You need to make their work easier. You need to prep enough for the interview, to document in writing the things you see that you can affect. You need to give them no alternative but to hire you.

Rosanna was interested in a posting on Monster.com for a regional director of business operations position with a national healthcare firm. She succeeded in receiving an interview with the hiring manager. She never heard from the firm again, and to her the opportunity was lost. After researching, we learned that this happened to her:

When she was granted the interview, Rosanna was excited. She dressed professionally and was very courteous. She was punctual. She was even quite qualified and had a strong résumé. The hiring manager, Paul Taylor, was very interested in meeting her.

Rosanna arrived and began chatting with Paul about the position and business in general. Paul lost some interest in Rosanna as a lead candidate because although he thought she was bright, he was not convinced she was a perfect "fit." Rosanna answered all the questions about her past accomplishments but did not demonstrate a solid understanding of the industry, key business drivers, and how she would enable the company to meet its key objectives.

She did not initiate a discussion about the firm's business challenges. She did not discuss the challenges facing the industry or demonstrate that she had researched the firm's key competitors or customers. She did not show up with a written work or business plan. She was a solid candidate and remained a solid number two draft choice. She did not get the position.

Another candidate, David, arrived for the interview having completed lengthy research on the company and having developed a business plan draft to discuss. Paul said later that both candidates were probably equally qualified but that David demonstrated more effort and creativity. Paul expected that to translate into more of those qualities on the job.

Paul: "Both candidates were amply qualified: good schools, career path, Fortune 500 pedigrees, well spoken. In fact, going into the interview I was probably expecting Rosanna to be a closer hit based on the two résumés. But David showed up with a credible attempt at a business plan, one that at least demonstrated that he understood our business, challenges, and objectives and how he would get us there. It's one thing to talk about it and another to prove it. Every interview question that came up, David spun the answer around how he would be a solution for us, as opposed to Rosanna communicating what she did in the past."

A proactive approach to interviewing is to think with a hiring manager's mindset. Prepare to do this by reading the job posting thoroughly—not just what is written but what is implied. Also, do some reconnaissance work on the company and the position. During the interview listen for clues in the questions you're asked and the issues that are discussed. Your comments and questions will let the interviewer know that you have an understanding of what's needed to do the job and that you are the solution to his or her problem.

How the Assessment Process Works

For employers, hiring right the first time is essential because:

- The cost of a wrong hire is tremendous.
- The benefit of getting it right is enormous.

Employers that recognize this go to great lengths to match the right people to the right job. Selection is a two-way process in which both you and the hiring company make a choice. That choice should be right for both of you.

From one company to another, hiring practices can differ as much as the products they sell. Can you imagine similar hiring practices at IBM and Ben and Jerry's? In broad outline form, though, there are commonalities. The selection process may involve several stages. Each stage is designed to weed out and reduce the candidate pool until the right candidate is selected.

1. Traditionally this first step involves sending in your résumé. You cannot overemphasize the importance of your résumé. Your résumé can make or break this step, depending on your level of sponsorship in the company. When this process is happening behind closed doors, you must make certain that your résumé will not stop you from getting to the next level.
2. In large organizations, the short list of candidates who move on from step 1 usually is set up through screening interviews by HR. Psychological or ability testing may occur at this stage too. This may include:
   - IQ testing
   - A personality and motivation questionnaire
   - Interest inventories
   - Simulation exercises

The number of candidates who get through the round will drop significantly. For some jobs in some companies, this will be the final stage.

3. The last step consists of final interviews with hiring managers and prospective peers.

Empathize: See Yourself Through Their Eyes

When you interview, your objective generally is to receive an offer. What is the objective of the interviewer? Is it to learn about you? The industry? The competition? The candidate pool out there now? To complete the requisite external interviews and justify hiring an internal candidate?

Generally, the hiring manager's objective for the interview is to hire the right candidate, and the second most common objective is the last one mentioned above—hiring an internal candidate. You need to find out what the reason is for the interview.

The interviewer generally is looking for three components of your candidacy: experience, aptitude and intelligence, and a gut reaction.

Experience is evaluated on your work history, positions held, the companies for which you've worked, salary levels, and specific skills. Your interviewing objective is to have your key messages for each of these areas prepared before the interview.

Here are three assessment elements of candidates:

- *Experience.* Do you have the work history desired? This is objective information and can be tilted in your favor if the gut reaction is favorable.
- *Basic intelligence.* The hiring manager must feel you are bright enough for the position. Psychological testing (discussed later in this chapter) can influence this element.
- *Gut reaction.* It must be in your favor or you're out. Many skilled and qualified candidates have not received offers because the hiring manager just did not feel right about them.

During the interview the interviewer will be looking for many other characteristics. Consider the previously described elements the foundation of the interview. The interviewer will ask questions to collect specific job-related information related to each of the job's key characteristics. Be prepared to answer questions relating to some of these key characteristics. They include the following:

Workshop 1

List your experiences so you have them prepped for the interview:

Work History

Employer	Position Held	Salary Level	Key Accomplishments/Skills

---

Characteristic	Considerations for You
Leadership	Prepare examples of times you've exhibited leadership. This is critical for a managerial or executive role.
Planning and organization	Complex situations that involved multiple components and possible outcomes.
Communication skills	Listening and written and oral communication and/or presentation.
Team player	Your ability to work with and through others to achieve department or company goals.

Continued

Ability to take responsibility	You need to crave it to get ahead and impress the interviewer.
Empathy/caring	Ability to understand the environment around you; also relates to working for the success of those around you, not just yours.
Positive, self-assured, confident, high self-esteem	Confidence is everything in all facets of life. People like to be around positive, vibrant, confident people.
Energy, drive, motivation, and appearance during the interview	Without being pushy or aggressive, you *must* demonstrate high energy, motivation, and enthusiasm.
Delegation/control	Managers need to be able to delegate but also need to maintain control of their domain.
Decision making	This includes both the ability (tangible, specific) and the capability to be a good decision maker.
Strong work ethic	After many different corporate scandals you can understand the relevance of this.
Development of self and others, ability to motivate others	You have to make others successful to be successful.
Initiative	Show them you are not the type of person who needs to be told what to do. Be action-oriented and make things happen.

Follow the Leader

When you speak, the interviewer will listen for indications that you are not responding to the questions he or she asks. This happens all the time to people in conversations: someone will ask a question, and the response will be only slightly related to the question. *Stay on track*. Respond to the question and then ask the interviewer if he or she was satisfied that you answered what was asked.

> **TIP**
>
> Give examples of things you did and situations you encountered. It is your responsibility to educate the interviewer about your accomplishments. Sell yourself and share your experience. Then ask the interviewer if that sufficiently answered any questions. Give the interviewer a reason to move you to the next round of interviews.

Effective managers usually hire right the first time and experience low turnover. Managers who can identify the top performers when interviewing many job applicants position themselves, their team, and the company for long-term success. By being knowledgeable about the company you are interviewing with, being prepared to answer questions, and showing what makes you stand out among your peers, you increase the company's level of interest in you and increase your chance of getting the job.

Workshop 2

Imagine these are the areas about which you will be questioned. These questions represent both broad and specific areas. Whether you are asked about these things specifically or not, answering these questions on paper will make you well prepared and confident for the interview.

Question Area	Prepped Response
Critical thinking/analytical skills/problem solving/decision making	
Discuss a complex problem.	
What was your overall effectiveness?	
What process did you use to solve the problem? Show your logic.	
Interpersonal communication	
Do you communicate effectively?	
How do you exercise self-control and show respect, especially when things get hot?	
How are you going to establish rapport with the interviewer?	

Continued

Managerial and leadership ability	
Think strategically about good examples.	
Did you ever have to confront someone to get something done?	
What are groups and teams looking for in a leader?	
When are you a leader? When are you not?	
How have you had to exercise your authority? The outcome?	
Career motivation: Why this industry? Why this company?	
Know your short- and long-term goals.	
Be able to articulate the experiences that have influenced your career choices.	
Team skills	
Be humble about yourself and your decisions. Be able to adapt.	
Not rigid in your thinking	
Be flexible when working with others when you are either the leader or a group member.	
What are your most important contributions?	
What did you learn about yourself?	

Intellectual ability		
Be willing to take psychological and academic tests.		
Show expertise on the subject matter.		
Good citizenship		
Looking for someone who is a good person and has community interests. This can be important at some companies.		
Writing sample		
Show samples of work you've done.		
Have you thought about a business plan (see Chapter 19)?		

Psychological Tests

Aptitude and intelligence evaluations are less objective than work history. Here the interviewer bases his or her opinion on your intelligence as measured in several different ways, including how you fared in professional psychological assessments or similar third-party testing, how well spoken you are, how concise you are, and what your background and your education are.

Professional third-party testing (psychological testing) is very common. There are firms all over the country that perform such testing. Usually, this is a combination of a professional interview, computer testing, and perhaps old-fashioned multiple-choice and problem-solving questionnaires. The objective testing done through computer testing or written testing is the most common because it is standardized. It's easier to get information from tests than from an interview, and it is more consistent than information from a clinical interview. Finally, it is harder to get away with misleading information on a test than it is in an interview. Many tests have multiple "alarms" that go off when a test taker tries to lie. Also, some tests, such as the Rorschach ("inkblot test"), don't even give a clue about what preferred, or healthy, responses might be, and so it's pretty much impossible to fabricate a deceptive answer.

The biggest challenge in psychological tests is their ability to measure what they are supposed to measure. The accuracy, or usefulness, of a test is known as its validity. For example, suppose you wanted to develop a test to determine which of several job applicants would work well in sales. Would an arithmetic test be a valid test of job success? Not if the job required other skills, such as interpersonal skills. Many companies have used the same test for years. In that case they have accumulated statistics on how the preemployment testing matches with the long-term success and longevity of the employee. This is where tests are given the most credence.

For example, a prominently known Fortune 50 telecommunications company has used the same psychological test for years for new-hire senior salespeople and sales managers. When an employee does not "pass" the test, meaning the test indicates a person with skills that differ from the profile, the company almost never hires that person, even if he or she has a stellar track record and interview. Because the test has had a relative accuracy of over 80 percent, it becomes the most important part of the advanced interview process.

The sole reason for using psychological tests is to answer the question, "Should we accept this person or not?" Since psychological tests aren't magic, mistakes will be made. Even when a qualified psychologist makes a decision based on all the available evidence, there still will be doubts and shadows of doubts. Thus, a false-negative mistake occurs when a person truly qualified for a job is rejected; a false-positive mistake occurs when a person not truly qualified for a job is accepted.

When you are disqualified from a job application for psychological reasons, it means that there are things about your behavior and attitudes that are of concern to the psychologist evaluating you.

Those things are in contrast to the pattern of known success to which the company has subscribed. Usually if a psychological test turns against you, there is no recourse legally or professionally. Consider it a kiss of career death at that company.

Psychological tests fall into several categories:

- Achievement and aptitude tests are usually seen in educational and employment settings. They attempt to measure either how much you know about a certain topic (i.e., your achieved knowledge), such as math or spelling, or how much of a capacity you have (i.e., your aptitude) to master material in a particular area, such as logical relationships.
- Intelligence tests attempt to measure intelligence, or your basic ability to understand the world around you, assimilate its functioning, and apply that knowledge to enhance the quality of your life—in short, to determine if you "get it."
- Occupational tests attempt to match your interests with the interests of persons in known professions. The logic here is that if the things that interest you match up with, say, the things that interest most schoolteachers, you might make a good schoolteacher.
- Personality tests attempt to measure your basic personality style.

Comparing Candidates

Interviews

Interviews are still the most common method of assessment for selection. Interviews give both candidate and employer a chance to meet face-to-face, allowing both parties to question each other. They also rely on the interviewer's accurate recording and interpretation of the details you provide. This gets to the point we discussed earlier about staying on track and remaining focused.

Whatever the type of interview, interviewers probably will take notes as the interview goes along. You usually will be given an opportunity to ask questions at the end and will need to be prepared to talk about past and present experiences.

- *Competency-based interviews* focus on particular areas of competence important to the job and are clearly related to the job in question. The questions relate to particular abilities or styles: "Tell me about a time when you had to meet a tight deadline. How did you cope? What was the outcome?" You will need to come up with lots of examples of situations from your work experience, leisure activities, or home life.
- *Biographical interviews* are the most traditional format. They focus on the kind of information you might put on a résumé, such as work experience, educational background, leisure interests, circumstances (e.g., the kind of working hours and conditions you can manage), career goals, and an evaluation of your past accomplishments. The link between the questions and the job you're applying for may not be apparent.
- *Situational interviews* ask you to imagine yourself in a hypothetical situation and then ask what you would do. The situations may be taken directly from the job or may be more general.

Here are some common categories that hiring managers use when comparing candidates.

Interests

Interests refer to your personal preference for specific types of job-related activities in a wide range of occupations—for example, if you like working externally with customers, like doing back-office work, or like working with reports and analysis.

Personality Tests

Professional psychological testing enhances the quality and quantity of information available to employers making selection or promotion decisions. These tests maximize the benefit for employers in their selection procedures and, from the candidates' point of view, promote fairness and equality of opportunity.

Personality questionnaires look at behavioral style and how individuals like to work, as well as mental capacity. These questionnaires are not concerned with your technical learned abilities but with how you see yourself in terms of your personality, for example, the way you relate to others and your feelings and emotions.

It is becoming more common for employers to look at style in the recruitment process. That can help them plan development programs and place people within groups.

This personality assessment is based on the typologies identified by Carl Jung, who identified different personality types; subsequent researchers developed 16 personality types from his original work. These types are based on the following polarities:

Extrovert (E) versus introvert (I)

Sensory (S) versus intuitive (N)

Thinking (T) versus feeling (F)

Perception (P) versus judgment (J)

On completion of this assessment, you will be provided with a report that identifies your personality type and traits. Careers matching your personality profile also will be described in detail.

The definitions below give a brief explanation of what each personality type signifies. You can locate the detailed tests by contacting a psychological testing company; there are many in every major market. You may also find good testing information by searching Internet websites.

Extroverted Types

ESFJ Personality Type

As well as being directed toward external phenomena, you are responsive to sensory, feeling, and organizational factors.

- Counselors, childcare workers, social workers

ENTP Personality Type

You think well and intuitively, as well as making perceptive decisions about the outer world.

- Photographers, salespersons, journalists

ESTJ Personality Type

Your personality is particularly focused on thinking as well as being oriented toward external, sensory, and organizational matters.

- Financial managers, supervisors

ESFP Personality Type

You are good at adjusting to new situations in a feeling manner as well as being sensitive and outer directed.

- Childcare workers, secretaries, counselors

ESTP Personality Type

As well as being able to adjust to new situations, you think carefully about your responses to the world.

- Builders, plumbers, carpenters

ENFP Personality Type

You are an intuitive, feeling, perceptive person who is oriented toward the world around you.

- Actors, musicians, teachers

ENTJ Personality Type

As well as being an intuitive and organized person with an orientation toward the world, you make thoughtful decisions.

- Lawyers, managers, operations researchers

ENFJ Personality Type

You are organized, intuitive, and outer directed and rely on feelings a great deal.

- Counselors, teachers, home economists

Introverted Types

ISFJ Personality Type

You are a well-grounded person who gets on well with people and deals with everyday issues in an organized way.

- Teachers, health workers, librarians

ISTJ Personality Type

As well as having good self-acceptance, you are reflective, organized, and focused on the world around you.

- Accountants, engineers, technicians

ISFP Personality Type

You adjust well to new situations and relate through your feelings. You are responsible and respond well to sensory factors.

- Stock clerks, outdoor workers, painters

INTP Personality Type

In addition to being intuitive and well grounded, you think things out carefully before making decisions that are based on your own perceptions.

- Scientists, engineers, writers

INFP Personality Type

You adjust well to new situations. You relate through feelings and intuition. You are well grounded and trust in yourself.

- Editors, psychologists, artists

INFJ Personality Type

Your intuitions go hand in hand with your self-acceptance. You are strong on the feeling and organizational dimensions.

- Psychiatrists, teachers, writers

ISTP Personality Type

You think deeply as you adjust to new situations, and you are well grounded and respond to the world in an ongoing way.

- Craft workers, statisticians, technicians

INTJ Personality Type

Thoughtful reflections, intuition, organized strategies, and autonomy are key dimensions of your personality orientation.

- Engineers, scientists, social scientists

Motivation Questionnaires

Motivation questionnaires look at the factors that drive you to perform well at work. Areas that may be considered include the energy with which you approach tasks, how long and under what circumstances your effort will be maintained, and the situations that increase and decrease your motivation.

Motivation is a dimension of a person-job fit that is used most often in development situations once you are in a job, but it also may be used in recruitment.

Your motivating drivers also can be ascertained through testing. Unless the testing is done solely to gauge your personality, most management psychological tests will attempt to uncover your primary drivers.

Ability Tests

These tests look at the extent to which you are able to carry out various aspects of a job. They focus on a variety of skills with varying levels of difficulty.

Often employers are interested in your ability to do a task. In this case they may use assessment methods that aim to simulate aspects of that task. Alternatively, they may choose to assess more generic skills, such as interpersonal communication and the ability to make decisions on the basis of written information, which will predict how well you may do the task.

Apart from ability tests, there are many ways in which employers may try to assess ability in selection procedures. Employers may be looking for particular abilities or skills they expect you to have already. These skills may be quite specific, such as using a particular programming language or knowing when to use different types of equations. These kinds of skills are likely to have been gained during your education or work experience, and so employers may consider them by using the following.

Simulation Exercises

Simulation exercises are designed to replicate a particular task or skill needed for a job. They are usually specific in nature, targeted to that which is required to be successful in the role for which you are interviewing. Simulation exercises can be fun if you do not stress out too much. The tasks and skills that may be assessed differ widely, and so there is considerable variation in the kinds of materials, scenarios, and people involved from exercise to exercise. Different types of simulation exercise include:

- Presentations
- In-baskets
- Tests of productive thinking
- Group exercises
- Fact-finding exercises
- Role plays

Presentations

Presentations are very common in sales and public relations. You may be asked to make a formal presentation to a number of interviewers. In some cases this will mean preparing a presentation in advance on a given topic. In other cases you may be asked to interpret and analyze information and present a case to support a decision. For example, you are asked to prepare a sales presentation on anything from selling a paper clip to making a formal sales presentation on the hiring company's product based on your own research. The latter is much more challenging. These presentations usually last 5 to 15 minutes.

In-Baskets

In-baskets involve working from the contents of a manager's in-basket, which typically consist of letters, memos, and background information. You may be asked to deal with paperwork and make decisions, balancing the volume of work against a tight schedule.

For example, you are asked to take over the role of marketing manager for a company organizing a trade event. Your tasks are based on organizing the booth and touching on disciplines including personnel, finance, and marketing.

Tests of Productive Thinking

These tests look at the volume, diversity, and originality of your ideas. You are presented with open-ended questions that pose various problems and situations. You are asked to generate responses within a time limit. For example, you may be given a scenario in which the finance group has expressed low job satisfaction and staff turnover is high. You are asked to generate as many ideas as you can for ways to increase staff morale within a limited budget.

Group Exercises

Group exercises are timed discussions in which a group of participants work together to tackle a work-related problem. Sometimes you are given a particular role on a team, such as the sales manager or personnel manager. Other times no roles are allocated. You are observed by assessors who are looking not for whether you are giving right or wrong answers but for how you interact with your colleagues on the team.

For example, you are asked to role-play a member of the marketing team for a telecommunications company. The team is required to discuss the launch of a new product. You may have to make decisions or recommendations on advertising, ethical concerns, packaging, and pricing.

Fact-Finding Exercises

In a fact-finding exercise you may be asked to reach a decision with only partial knowledge. Your task may be to decide what additional information you need to make the decision and sometimes also to question the interviewer to obtain that information.

For example, you are asked to take on the role of a regional manager in a healthcare company dealing with a customer complaint. You are asked to decide what further information you need to reach a decision, and you have a time limit in which you can question the assessor to obtain that information before presenting your fully reasoned argument.

Role Plays

In a role play you are given a particular role to assume for a certain task. The task will involve dealing with a role player in a certain way, and there will be an assessor watching. More on this in Chapter 8.

For example, you are asked to take on the role of a new manager in an automotive company, and as part of the induction program you are required to have a meeting with a dealer you would be supporting. You need to introduce yourself and find out if the dealer has any issues that need sorting out. If there are, you need to explain to the dealer your approach to resolving them.

Case Interview Approaches

Typically utilized by consulting firms, a case interview evaluates a candidate's analytical skills. The interviewer presents you with a real or simulated problem to consider. Several different kinds of cases may be presented in an interview setting. The two most typical kinds are numerical cases and actual or theoretical questions. Below are some examples of case study questions.

Sample Methodology Questions

- How many convenience stores are there in New York City?
- How many cars are produced in Detroit each year?
- How many football teams are there in the NCAA?
- How much is a Super Bowl advertisement worth?
- How many hamburgers are consumed each day in America?

The goal in asking an estimation question is not to see whether you are an expert in these industries. Your logical thought process and approach to problem solving are of interest. Rather than compute an answer in your head, you are encouraged to "talk out" your approach to the problem step-by-step.

Another type of case question is an actual or theoretical client situation. These cases may be presented in a written or a verbal format.

TIPS

Here are some tips if you encounter this approach in an interview:

1. *Buy time—clarify the question.* After listening carefully to the case description, clarify the question by repeating it back to the interviewer or ask questions to clarify the case. Make sure you understand all the facts.

2. *Structure your response.* Once you understand the case, identify key issues and organize your response. Refer to the SAR approach in Chapter 13. Your approach is the most important part of the answer. Be concise and focused. Do not talk in circles, and don't talk until you're ready.

3. *Analyze issues and test hypotheses.* Discuss potential findings, present alternatives, and present hypotheses for future testing and discussion. You can use a sketch here (i.e., a matrix or flowchart) if it is helpful.
4. *Summarize the case.* Be logical in your response.
5. *Use questions like those listed here or think up your own.* Then practice how you would answer and solve hypothetical business problems. It can be fun.

General Business Questions

- A couple of college students want to quit school to start a dot-com company. What should they consider before doing that?
- Ford Motor is not selling enough cars. What would you suggest it should do?
- A record label is considering signing a new music act. What should the company consider before signing it?

As in methodology questions, be prepared to talk out your thought process.

On the Hiring Manager's Side: Decision-Making Styles

Did you ever go on a first date and think it went great? You are sure it will lead to a relationship; this is the one! Then you call the next day, leave a message, and get no return call. Then no call for another day, then a week, and then you hear from a friend of a friend that that person is not interested. The same thing can happen in interviewing. Sometimes you can be sure that you hit a home run and struck up a great rapport with the interviewer but never hear from the company again.

Although you were able to evaluate the interviewer's communication style, you may have erred in estimating the decision-making style. The decision-making style is not exclusive to the employment process, nor does it affect interviewers only. Everyone has his or her own decision-making style, and it reflects on all areas of life. The four decision-making styles are as follows:

- *Pragmatic.* A *pragmatic decision maker* will tend to be very businesslike and formal and possibly difficult to read. He is bottom-line oriented and wants only the relevant facts needed to make a decision. He makes very quick, rational decisions. A take-charge individual, the *pragmatic* person will control the interview whether you think so or not. He is all business, firm but fair. He wants the facts quickly and makes hiring decisions the same way.
- *High energy.* The *high-energy decision maker* is emotional, extroverted, and inspired. Liked by many, she is prone occasionally to step on a few toes. She is always on the go, loves to talk, enjoys being the center of attention, makes quick decisions, and has a short attention span. She's highly competitive and accepts the consequences of her actions, good or bad. During the interview the *high-energy* person is enthusiastic and makes you feel good. She loves to talk and tells you all the great things the company does, often getting carried away with herself. She may start one sentence and finish with another. She is surprisingly competent and has a personality to make the best of any situation.
- *Congenial.* The *congenial decision maker* is concerned about and wants to be liked by everyone. She is happiest pleasing others and avoids direct conflict. She does not like confrontation or high pressure. Her decision making is erratic. During the interview the *congenial* person wants everyone to win and be happy. She wants to hire everybody and does not like to hurt anyone's feelings. If you are not selected for the job, she may feel uncomfortable calling you with bad news. As a result, you keep waiting for a decision that already has been made because this hiring manager experiences grave trepidations in delivering bad news.

■ *Analytical.* Slow, cautious, and surefooted, the *analytical decision maker* is in no hurry to make decisions. He loves analyzing, reviewing, and evaluating data. He works slowly, goes by the book, and wants all the facts and figures before making a decision. He is not sensitive to his environment or to people. During the employment interview the *analytical* person can be unyielding and obstinate. He tends not to make a decision if there is any risk of making an incorrect one.

Prepare in advance how you might approach each interview, depending on each of these styles. This will help you tailor your approach methodically rather than make it up on the fly.

What Employers Are Looking For

The ad looks like the perfect fit:

Vice President, Marketing. That may even be your current title.

Help make us an industry leader in an exciting, rapid-growth business. That sounds pretty good too.

Take-charge manager with excellent people and organizational skills. "That's me again," you think, "and I can back it up."

Must have at least nine years' experience. Got it!

In the marketing of consumer home products. "Ugh, it was all good up until now . . ."

You've been marketing for consumer electronics and enter-tainment for a satellite (cable) television system. The prospective employer is about the same size as your current company, and your marketing organization would be about the same size. But the job calls for experience in this specific industry. You don't have it, and so you move on.

Hold on there. You may be able to salvage this opportunity if you understand why potential employers require experience in their field or industry. A similar background is important because it decreases the company's risk. If you've succeeded in the same field, you'll probably replicate your achievements for the new employer. If you have same-industry experience, you can add value sooner because your ramp-up time will be much shorter.

Shift the Focus from Experience to Expertise

There is a big difference between expertise and experience. It's the difference between someone who has had 15 years of experience playing tennis at a club level and Andre Agassi, an all-time great and expert in the field. Experience does not necessarily differentiate you; expertise does.

Expertise isn't interchangeable from candidate to candidate. Years of experience might be considered interchangeable in com-paring candidates' résumés. Specific credentials also might be con-sidered interchangeable. You need to project that you are the Andre Agassi of your field, an expert rather than a journeyman who has put in her or his time.

Often when potential employers say they're looking for experience, they're actually seeking expertise. They prefer to hire not someone with knowledge of the position's key subject matter but someone with vision and the ability to accomplish goals. Employers usually are impressed by credentials (degrees, certifications, etc.), which prove you're familiar with the job's technical dimensions.

Some fields, such as medicine, engineering, public accounting, and software development, require significant subject-matter expertise for an applicant even to be considered for employment. In hundreds of other areas, the necessary knowledge can be picked up "on the fly."

In these cases you don't have to be an expert to land the job. Show you're a "quick study," and the employer may expect that you will acquire the necessary technical skill soon after you're hired.

Most management competencies reflect transferable abilities, not technical expertise. Think of a few classic examples:

- Motivating employees.
- Troubleshooting problems.
- Keeping one's head when those about one lose theirs.
- Translating goals into practical priorities.
- Inspiring trust and confidence in superiors, peers, and staff.
- Organizing people, information, and activities.
- Setting and applying performance standards.

General managers typically are valued for their ability to oversee and manage a variety of tasks and functions that they don't know how to perform themselves. The chief operating officer doesn't need to know how to install a networked computer system to manage the information services department.

In marketing your transferable abilities, you're demonstrating that you can apply experience gained in one setting to a different environment. When a president recruits a new cabinet member, he doesn't focus on technical skills ("Have you ever been a secretary of homeland defense before?"). Instead, he looks for good judgment, a good track record, maturity, and street smarts that have been demonstrated in other roles.

Career Changers

The distinction between expertise and experience is critical to career shifters. If you hope to change your work role or setting significantly, you have two options:

1. Acquire a new set of technical skills ("recredential yourself").
2. Market your experience as transferable into a new setting.

In general, once you've reached midcareer, it's easier to apply the second strategy. But both present considerable risk, which is one reason why a major career shift should never be taken lightly.

Let's return to the ad from the consumer home products company. Keeping in mind the distinction between experience and expertise, it's not always practical for employers to demand that candidates have direct experience that's identical, not just equivalent, to the position being filled. In fact, if they insist that applicants have relevant expertise, they may not have the opportunity to identify the best talent, particularly if technical competency can be acquired on the job. Overly demanding hiring criteria actually may diminish the pool of well-qualified candidates.

Another problem emerges when the screening requirement is keyed to length of experience. Does "six to eight years of experience" refer to a floor ("You must have at least . . ."), a ceiling ("no more than . . ."), or a pricing standard ("We've got $92,000 to spend. How much experience can we buy for that?")? To avoid being screened out for being underqualified or overqualified, try to uncover the type and level of experience the employer seeks.

Next, focus on emphasizing the parts of your employment background that are most similar to those for the prospective position. Ask yourself this question: if the employer succeeded in hiring the kind of experiences he claims to want, what specific behaviors and capabilities would the candidate demonstrate?

To make a case that your experience is functionally equivalent to the employer's needs, you must review the rest of the job description. From it, try to pull out specific functional skills the position requires and then identify accomplishments in your work history that demonstrate your ability to add value in those areas.

It's easier to communicate the equivalence of your transferable abilities when you are talking directly with a hiring manager rather than writing a response to an ad. Most ad replies are read first by screeners—not hiring managers—whose job is to weed out as many applicants as possible. For them, mechanically matching words in the ad to those in the response is safest; they may not have enough authority or expertise to judge what constitutes an acceptable substitute.

Review the exercise in Chapters 2 and 10 of *202 Great Resumes*. Take time to review 8 to 10 key accomplishments. You'll find quite an inventory of transferable abilities.

For each major accomplishment, analyze the situation, your activities, and the outcomes, asking yourself what strengths and abilities they require. From this exercise you can develop a list of action verbs and personal qualities that are strongly supported by your work history.

Finally, identify the transferable abilities that most closely match the employer's needs. Whether replying to an ad or making your points in a face-to-face meeting, you must show that the employer's actual requirements are functionally equivalent to your strengths. Your mission is to demonstrate that what's needed isn't the specified experience but *your* experience.

Core Competencies Employers Are Looking For

Employers often describe jobs in terms of required competencies, a combination of "behaviors" that lead to superior performance in a role. The principal components include:

- *Personal style.* How you relate to your colleagues, team, and organization. Demonstrates flexibility when working with colleagues who have competing points of views and different types of experience in order to find solutions that work. Maintains good relationships during the collaborative process.
- *Motivation.* Your initiative; your drive to problem-solve and create. Creates new and imaginative approaches to work-related issues. Identifies fresh approaches and shows a willingness to question traditional assumptions.
- *Knowledge.* Specific, objective skills you've acquired; information required to perform in the job. Understands technical or professional aspects of work and continually maintains technical knowledge.
- *Aptitude.* What you are capable of doing.

What Skills Should You Showcase?

Some skills are highly specific and require specialist training. However, the general skills and abilities employers look for, usually referred to as transferable skills, are those that can be developed in one place or company and applied to a new position.

Examples of Transferable Skills

- *Decision making.* Identifying options, evaluating them, and then choosing the most appropriate ones.
- *Problem solving.* Identifying and using an appropriate method or technique to arrive at a solution:
  - Think critically and act logically to evaluate situations, solve problems, and make decisions.
  - Understand and solve problems involving mathematics and use the results.
  - Use technology, instruments, tools, and information systems effectively.
  - Access and apply specialized knowledge from various fields (e.g., skilled trades, technology, physical sciences, arts, and social sciences).
- *Planning.* Working out how to schedule available resources and activities to meet an objective.
- *Ability to prioritize.* Being able to decide priorities for achieving targets.
- *Information technology literacy.* Understanding and being able to use a range of software, such as word processing, spreadsheets, and databases.
- *Teamwork.* Working effectively with others to achieve objectives.
- *Oral communication.* Using speech to express ideas and give information or explanations effectively.
- *Adaptability.* Changing or modifying behavior in response to the needs, wishes, or demands of others.
- *Quantitative analysis.* Having the ability to use and understand numbers.
- *Written communication.* Producing grammatical, well-expressed, easily understood, and interesting text:
  - Understand and speak the languages in which business is conducted.

- Listen to understand and learn.
- Read, comprehend, and use written materials, including graphs, charts, and displays.
- Write effectively in the languages in which business is conducted.
- *Leadership.* Being able to lead and motivate, set direction, and win the commitment of others.
- *Business awareness.* Having an interest in and knowledge of the commercial environment.
- *Time management.* Managing personal tasks effectively and meeting deadlines.

Written Evaluations

Below is a sample evaluation form a company might use. Depending on the level of the position for which you are interviewing, there may be multiple interviews with multiple individuals. There are many examples of candidates being required to complete over five different interviews for a position. That can include peer interviews, where potential peers will spend 15 to 30 minutes with a candidate to evaluate him or her. These are usually easier interviews because they are more casual. Your objective is to avoid letting your guard down.

Example of Internal Candidate Evaluation Form I

Interviewer: _____   Interviewee: _____

Please indicate your evaluation of an applicant by checking the appropriate boxes below.

Appearance	Outstanding	Good	Average	Poor
Personality/demeanor	( )	( )	( )	( )
Self-confidence	( )	( )	( )	( )
Maturity	( )	( )	( )	( )
Communication skills/ articulation of views	( )	( )	( )	( )
Dedication to work	( )	( )	( )	( )

Continued

Extracurricular activities	( )	( )	( )
Academic achievements	( )	( )	( )
Work experience	( )	( )	( )
Overall impression	( )	( )	( )

(1) Strong candidate: Recommend for immediate hiring

(2) Good candidate: Have no reservations regarding hiring

(3) Marginal candidate: Have reservations regarding hiring (please comment below)

(4) Weak candidate: Should not be considered further for hiring (please comment below)

Sample In-House Evaluation Form II

Personality	strong			weak		
personable	1	2	3	4	5	abrasive
enthusiastic	1	2	3	4	5	lifeless
Verbal Expression						
articulate	1	2	3	4	5	difficult to understand
quick to respond	1	2	3	4	5	unresponsive
expression organized	1	2	3	4	5	disjointed thought
Personal Development						
confident	1	2	3	4	5	insecure
exhibits self-control	1	2	3	4	5	undisciplined
assertive	1	2	3	4	5	passive

Strongly Favor   Favor   Acceptable   Opposed   Strongly   Opposed

Look these forms over. Look at each dimension and how you could be evaluated. Practice a way to demonstrate each of these dimensions in the interview so that you will come off favorably.

The Transformation: Trends for 2014 and Beyond

Remote employees, changes in healthcare (from the employer perspective), communications enabling outsourcing overseas, business driven by social media, buying behaviors moving online, search engine optimization, and Google requiring expertise in managing the online presence to survive—these are all very drastic changes to business survival in just the last two to three years. Since the time that we wrote the previous edition of this book in 2004, Circuit City closed, and, even with that, Best Buy has had to change its business model. Thousands of jobs are being outsourced, and many more employees work at home. To survive and grow, we're all required to be more flexible and nimble.

This is exciting and can provide opportunities for you. You have to recognize that and represent yourself as current and part of this evolution, as dynamic and part of that change. The research techniques we reviewed will help you identify how your target company is positioned and how you fit. Here's how to do that.

> **TIPS**
>
> ■ Employees need to be visionary.
> ■ Employees need to become change agents.
> ■ Employees need to be resilient.
> ■ Employees need to problem-solve.

Becoming a Visionary

Being a visionary tends to be one of those innate qualities that is difficult to learn. Why is it that some people have large amounts of imagination and others have less? Why do some people seem to have natural leadership aptitude and others seem not to? I think that the broader one's experiences, the more one reads; and the more one thinks concretely about the future, the more likely it is that whatever visionary aptitude one has will be nurtured. The other interesting point is that often the one who appears to be a visionary is simply the person who has the moxie to "get it done." With no disrespect to Michael Dell, the concept of selling personal computers directly to end users is not exceedingly visionary. But the execution that he envisioned is superb, and the confidence he had that he could succeed showed more courage than many with a similar idea would have had.

- Seek out opportunities. Represent that you are the type who sees what is happening, what is not happening, and what can be done about it. You need to understand your customer and the end customer and how you fit into the picture.
- You need to create a compelling picture of the future for yourself, your team, and your customers.
- You need to be a key that links today with tomorrow. You need to understand the big picture.

Becoming a Change Agent

Why take the risk of winding up in the crosshairs of office politics? Here are three good reasons:

- *Survival.* Sometimes you can see that the company needs to change and that if someone doesn't inspire that change, that person will be out of a job. This is a great motivator for shaking things up: do it or line up for unemployment. The same reasoning justifies joining that organization. The organization may need you in order to survive or to get to the next level.
- *Recognition.* By inspiring change in the organization, you risk raising a few hackles. But if things go well, others will take notice. You'll be known not as Dan Schmitz, product manager, but as Dan Schmitz, the guy who helped the company stay afloat.
- *Fortune.* If the changes you inspire lead to a new revenue stream and you've negotiated a cut for yourself or if you have a very stand-up employer, change may be very profitable. A change that can save money or make money usually is seen as a change for the better, and it's easily justifiable to executives and financial accounting types.

To be a change agent you need to do more than raise the issue; you need to propose a solution and, if possible, be part of that solution. You want to be seen as an innovator and a valuable contributor, not as a do-nothing whiner. If nobody's monitoring those patches, why not volunteer to do the job?

Not everyone in the organization may believe that change is inevitable and necessary. Some may use the "if it ain't broke" cliché. If you demonstrate that change may be profitable and back it up with hard facts, it becomes more difficult for senior management to push back. You need to exercise good judgment about when to play the change management card in the interview process.

Becoming Resilient

Resilience is the ability to recover from change or adjust to change easily or quickly. Resilient individuals exhibit the following five characteristics. You need to represent these characteristics in your interview and on the job.

- *Solutions oriented.* Display a desire to look for present or future opportunities rather than feeling insecure and uncomfortable about change.
- *Structured.* Use organized methods for dealing with change. (An example of this is in the Introduction—notice how we wrote out structured methodologies for approaching tasks, such as "How Do You Matrix-Manage?").
- *Visionary.* Know what needs to be achieved and be able to determine how to get there.
- *Adaptable.* Be flexible in responding to uncertainty and change.
- *Proactive.* Understand this is not really a word but a business term. *Active* is the proper term, with *inactive* being the opposite. You need to demonstrate initiative, to meet change and plan for it rather than wait for it to happen.

These tests can be fun. The results may be exactly how you see yourself, or perhaps you will be surprised. Either way, you should get a sense of the traits desirable to employers.

Workshop

Here is a fun exercise to test your resiliency.

1. Read each statement.
2. Assign a score to each statement based on how much you agree that the statement fits you.

   1 = not at all

   2 = a little

   3 = somewhat

   4 = to a great extent

   5 = very much

Section 1: Solutions Oriented	Score
1	I consider myself focused on solutions.	
2	I explore alternatives before settling on a solution to a problem.	
3	I create realistic solutions to problems when they are presented.	
4	I am creative when faced with problems.	
5	When faced with a challenge, I am confident I will find a solution.	
6	I engage in creative problem solving to create a plan.	
	Total for this section	

Section 2: Structured	Score
7	I anticipate change and plan for it.	
8	I execute plans consistently with the end result in mind.	
9	When I determine what to do, I identify the tactics I will use to accomplish my plan.	
10	I use company tools, processes, and systems to plan and implement change (*read:* I accomplish change by playing by the rules and doing the right things).	
11	When there is uncertainty, I use problem-solving techniques to identify what needs to be done.	
	Total for this section	

Section 3: Visionary — Score

12	I see the "big picture."	
13	I am strategic and methodical in my approach to changing a situation.	
14	I am goal oriented when dealing with change.	
	Total for this section	

Section 4: Adaptable — Score

15	I am flexible in times of uncertainty.	
16	My skills are varied and multifaceted so that I can easily adapt to change.	
17	During change I adjust to new circumstances.	
18	When discussing options, I am always open-minded about other ideas.	
	Total for this section	

Section 5: Proactive — Score

19	I tend to plan for change rather than react to change.	
20	I am more action oriented than most.	
21	Taking reasonable risks should be rewarded and encouraged.	
22	It is very important to stay in touch with customers.	
23	I spend a lot of time observing and interpreting trends so that I am prepared for the need to change.	
	Total for this section	

How Did You Do?

Category	Strength ☺	Acceptable ☺	Development Need ☹	Your Score
Solutions oriented	24–30	15–23	6–14	
Structured	20–25	13–19	5–12	
Visionary	12–15	8–11	3–7	
Adaptable	16–20	10–15	4–9	
Proactive	20–25	13–19	5–12	
Total score	92–115	59–87	23–54	

7

The Organizational Message Chart

WHEN I WAS in high school, I had a big paper and presentation to deliver in English. I worked hard on it and spent time at the library to research the topic: the Iran hostage crisis of 1979. When I finally delivered it, I was nervous. I knew the topic but had not prepped enough or created a concise outline to reference. I got a B.

That night my mom and dad asked me how it had gone. I told them. My dad knew I was expecting an A to be a slam-dunk. "What happened?" he asked. I told him that I lost focus in the delivery and that the spirit of my presentation was muddled. His response: "Don't you understand you need to prioritize your key points and then make sure everything else supports that one key message?"

That is the premise behind the Organizational Message Chart. You need to focus on your key point, support it, and not lose track along the way.

> That is how interviewing works too. You need to keep your most important message always at the forefront, and everything else you say should support your key point.

The Organizational Message Chart is a revolutionary technology for changing the way you think about preparing for interviews. This tool is simple to use and effective in building confidence so that you can interview at a peak-performance level. Successful candidates—the ones who get hired for the top jobs—do two things better than anyone else in an interview:

1. *Sell and deliver the "right" messages (value).*
   - Skills and abilities that have value
   - Credentials and qualifications that indicate value
   - Experience and a track record that demonstrate value
   - Achievements that provide evidence of value
   - Intangibles: other sources that provide additional evidence of value
2. *Present the messages in a powerful manner that builds rapport.*
   - With confidence
   - With professionalism
   - With intelligence
   - With class

The "Right" Information

The Organizational Message Chart helps you communicate the right information. The right information is the information that best addresses the questions "Why should I hire you?" "How can you best contribute to our goals and objectives?" and "What do you bring to the table that would help us economically or help us achieve our primary goals and objectives?"

> *I interviewed Robert for the position of company controller—a $110,000 job. Robert had all the skills and abilities to do the job, and the hiring process came down to two candidates: Robert and another candidate, Warren. We liked both candidates and thought both would be a good fit with our company and our corporate culture. Robert didn't get the job because even though he was at ease in the interview and interviewed well, Warren was able to better communicate what he would achieve.*

In other words, while Robert was telling us what his skills were and trying to persuade us that he was the right man for the job, Warren told us that our cash flow would be improved, our expenses would be reduced without compromising quality of service, and overall he would maintain and improve the financial health, vitality, and integrity of the company. He told us what we wanted to know—that he'd take care of our financial well-being and improve profits. In the end, Warren did a better job telling us what he would accomplish, while Robert simply told us what he had done. And there is a big difference between the two.

Daniel Graham, VP Finance
Smith and Cardinal Enterprises

And here's the exciting part about identifying the right messages: if you are confident that you have the right messages, you will be confident in your delivery and presentation style. Like a good sales professional, the more confident you are in your product (you), the more you believe in the product (you); and the more passionate and convincing you are when you promote the product (you), the more successful you will be in presenting the product and closing the deal!

Once you have identified the messages that answer the all-important question "Why should I hire you?" you will build an interviewing strategy around those messages!

Curly's "One-Thing" Formula

In the movie *City Slickers*, the tough cowboy and the seemingly "rough-around-the-edges" trail boss led a group of city folk who were going through a midlife crisis on a cattle drive. Curly (Jack Palance), the trail boss, was telling Mitch (Billy Crystal), one of those going through a midlife crisis, what his problem was. Curly said that Mitch was just like all the other city slickers who were trying to make sense of life. But the real meaning of life, according to Curly, all came down to just "one thing."

"What's that one thing, Curly?" Mitch asked with sincere interest as they rode their horses side by side back toward the campsite where the group was hunkering down for the evening. "You have to figure that out for yourself," Curly responded. "It's different for everyone."

> When it comes to winning the interview and securing the perfect job, it is best to determine the one message, above all others, that reigns supreme.

Curly's "one-thing" formula is that "the meaning of life all comes down to one thing," and everyone has to find out what that one thing is for himself or herself! When it comes to preparing for interviews, it would be best to identify, communicate, and accentuate the one message that has the most impact.

We call this the presidential message. You must identify that one presidential message for each prospective employer or manager before the interview. What is the most important message you can convey that will make the most difference? Once the presidential message is identified, you need only identify the six to eight supporting vice presidential messages that give credibility and validity to the presidential message. Then you build your interviewing strategy around those messages.

Value-Added Messages

The presidential message is the most important message that best answers the questions "Why should I hire you?" and "How will our company benefit by hiring you?" The VP messages are the critical messages that support the presidential message.

Value-added messages communicate the "added value" that a candidate brings to the job that "goes beyond the call of duty." They provide examples that lend credibility to the presidential message.

A Typical Corporate Organizational Chart

Let's get started by taking a look at a typical corporate organizational chart and seeing how we can modify it to become an Organizational Message Chart. Have you ever seen an organizational chart? You know, the chart with the president on top, the vice presidents below, the managers below that, and so on. It looks like a pyramid. Figure 7-1 shows a typical organizational chart.

The most important position on the chart in terms of economic value is the president. The vice presidents follow and then the rest of the gang.

If we wanted to turn this organizational chart into a powerful tool for identifying the core messages that would help us answer the question "Why should I hire you? What makes up your value that would benefit our company?" the chart might look something like Figure 7-2.

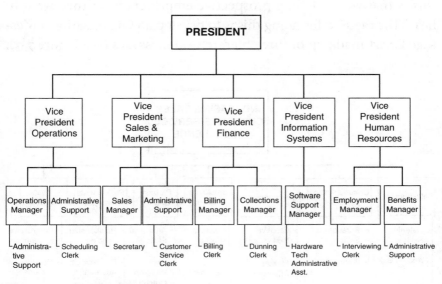

Figure 7-1 Organizational chart

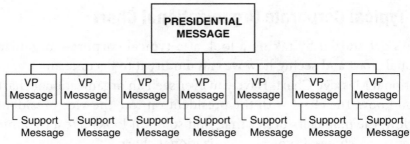

Figure 7-2 Core message chart

Template of Organizational Message Chart

Summary

The key to effective interviewing is that you meet with prospective employers and communicate what you can accomplish for them. We call this value messaging, or sending strategic messages that are "music to the prospective employer's ears." Another way of saying this is that we are telling prospective employers what they want to hear! The method for doing this is to develop an Organizational Message Chart made up of three hierarchical messages (see Figure 7-3).

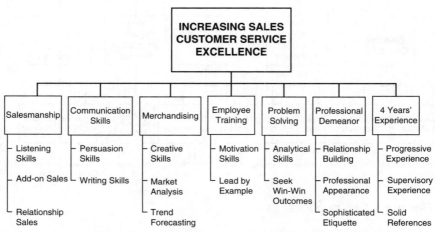

Figure 7-3 Organizational Message Chart with three hierarchical messages

The Hierarchy of Messages

1. Presidential message
2. Vice presidential messages (VP messages)
3. Support messages

Sample Organizational Message Chart

OMC Sample 1: Sixth-Grade Elementary School Teacher

To construct an OMC for a candidate seeking a position as a sixth-grade elementary school teacher, you begin, as always, with the question "Why should the school hire me?"

Presidential Message

To enhance the educational experience and prepare students for a rewarding life.

What skills, qualifications, and intangible assets do you offer that would indicate that you could indeed achieve the presidential message?

VP Message 1:	Improving reading scores
VP Message 2:	Improving math scores
VP Message 3:	Classroom management—discipline
VP Message 4:	Student-parent interface
VP Message 5:	Field trip and "real-life" education coordination
VP Message 6:	Curriculum enhancement
VP Message 7:	Three-time state delegate to the National Teacher's Conference, Washington, D.C.
Value-Added Message:	MBA, Library Science—able to improve library facilities *(a librarian is often a volunteer position in many elementary and middle schools)*

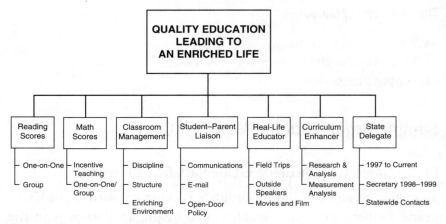

Figure 7-4 OMC 1: Sixth-grade elementary school teacher

See Figure 7-4, which illustrates the OMC for a sixth-grade elementary school teacher.

OMC Sample 2: Company President or CEO

To construct an OMC for a candidate seeking a position as a CEO or company president, you begin by asking the all-important question "Why should the company hire me?"

Presidential Message

To promote global expansion and enhance shareholder value and earnings

What skills, qualifications, and intangible assets do you offer that would indicate that you could indeed achieve the presidential message?

VP Message 1:   International corporate leadership

VP Message 2:   Reengineering and corporate restructuring

VP Message 3:   Mergers and acquisitions management

VP Message 4:   Organizational and personnel leadership

VP Message 5:   MBA: Oxford

VP Message 6:   Leadership role in building/directing four multimillion-dollar companies

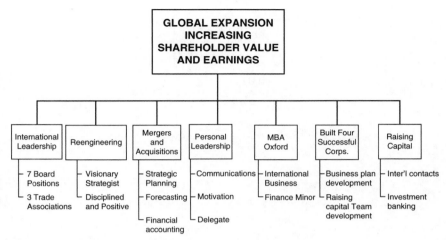

Figure 7-5 OMC 2: President or CEO

VP Message 7:   Highly experienced in raising capital for growth and expansion

Value-Added
Message: Key business and political contacts in 23 nations

See Figure 7-5, which illustrates an OMC for a corporate president or CEO.

8

Interview Preparation— Role Plays and Video

Personal Story

On the eve of my first interview for a director-level position with a Fortune 50 company, I took on an unpleasant preparation task. I wrote out about 15 questions I was sure the hiring vice president would ask. Then I called a colleague over to my house to help me rehearse. On the back porch on a warm Tampa evening, we sat around for two hours, with my friend asking question after question and I, the candidate, answering each. Then thinking about each answer, we did it all over again. The next day I nailed the interview with tight, concise answers that were on point with no extraneous clutter.

Candidate Story

In the spring of 2014, we interviewed Susan for a district manager position—1 of about 10 candidates in two days. We sat with candidate after candidate in an empty dining area of a Residence Inn. Midway through the meetings, Susan came in for her appointment: mid-30s, decent experience. She was wearing khaki pants and an untucked white shirt. She had some good experience; however, she did not dress for the role.

As she began telling us about herself, she volunteered a bunch of information, mostly personal and unnecessary—like consuming a bunch of empty calories. There was no way she was going to be a final candidate. So after 20 minutes, I stopped the interview and told her this position would not be a right fit for her. Of course, she was visibly upset, and I wanted to help her. I told her about some of the career guidance work we've done and offered some coaching, and I gave her some advice on her interview attire and her actual interviewing answers. And then I suggested she could prepare before an interview by role-playing with a friend, giving her tips and pointers on how to do that. By the end she was beaming and gave me a hug. She said she was going to nail the next interview she got.

Why Role-Play?

Have you read *Outliers* by Malcolm Gladwell or *The Talent Code* by Daniel Coyle? The point of both books is that excellence isn't God-given. Practice—deliberate practice—creates excellence. The list is huge, but people who become great at something get there through tons of hard, intentional work. The Beatles practiced thousands of hours before they ever had a hit record. Ronald Reagan is considered a great orator in American history, and he perfected that craft through years of acting and presenting. Even with kids, the best students and athletes are also the hardest working and those with the most mentoring help.

Role playing is really tough. I've taught several classes on interpersonal skills, coaching team members and performance management. In each class, the participants skill-practice principles that are built on communication skills, trust, delivering constructive criticism, and effective goal setting, with all participants buying in. You've never seen experienced professionals freeze or build up nerves like they do going into those first few role plays. But by the end of each class, you cannot even recognize the people from the beginning.

In leading a sales organization, really any organization, communication skills separate the leaders and all-stars from the rest. Everyone should role-play in preparation for an interview. Baseball players practice mundane grounders and fly balls for years, thousands for every ball touch in a game. After coaching kids in baseball for years, you hear the same things from parents after every game. "[Fill in the blank] had such a good game; you're so lucky to have him!" Somehow they never ask about how we practice, what drills we do, what practices we run with those "special" players.

It's not luck. It's the science of prep. It's about role playing and your rehearsal. Most candidates—and I really mean most, having interviewed hundreds of candidates—do not prep well or script out, even loosely, their responses. They wing it. Provide TMI. Not good!

"I'm Good"

When we start to discuss role playing, participants get uneasy. This has happened with candidates for interviews and team leaders in coaching. One person will always say up front, "I'm not good at role plays, but I'm really good at interviewing (or coaching a team member), so I'll be fine!" It's like a kid unable to field grounders in practice but telling us he could nail it in a real game. Or a presenter freezing up in rehearsals but reassuring us he will do great in the actual presentation. How you practice is how you will perform. Here are the steps you should follow to prepare to role-play for an interview:

ROLE-PLAYING STEPS

1. Take the job description and section off each competency as shown in the Introduction. Then bullet out your responses and alignment to each.
2. Section off three to five company areas as discussed in Chapter 1.
3. Enlist a friend to partner with you. Someone experienced in management and interviewing is ideal, but a peer could also work. You will want to get some coaching from your partner. Even if the person is not experienced enough to give feedback, you'll get a ton of improvement just by saying the words a few times.
4. Sit across from each other at a table. No distractions. If you need to get away, a hotel lobby area works great. Restaurants are often too full of distractions.

5. Run through the role play for at least four to six questions and answers (use the ones in Chapters 13–17 and customize them to the company job description) before stopping for feedback.
6. Take notes along the way next to the bullet points you've written out and refine along the way.

Your interviewer won't likely give you feedback on things like slowing down your speech, giving too much information, or representing or phrasing your employment gap or loss of employment. This is why it's helpful if your role-playing partner has some experience and is willing to give you some straight feedback. Don't take the constructive feedback personally, and if the focus is more on what you did wrong than what you did right, that's okay. Take the things you did wrong into account to improve your interviewing skills.

Video Makes Perfect

A professional golfer wants to improve her swing to reduce her handicap from 5 down to 0, so her golf pro video-records her swing to assess and enhance her technique. My son's baseball team video-records each player's swing and analyzes it against a professional's swing. We watch professional sports on television and, through the use of video technology, watch in slow motion the great plays and the miscues of professionals—all in an effort to understand and appreciate techniques (or lack of techniques) to understand and improve performance.

When political candidates are preparing to face the media or preparing for televised debates, they lock themselves in a hotel room with their coaches and advisors and practice, practice, practice, using video technology to ensure a winning performance.

But when it comes to average people seeking a job that will affect their careers and lives, video technology is seldom, if ever, used.

A winning strategy for acing the interview is using video technology to perfect technique, assuring confidence and mastery in the interview.

There are three primary advantages to incorporating video technology in preparing for an interview:

1. Assessing visual appearance
   - How do you dress? Is it appropriate for the kind of interview on which you are going?
   - How do you look physically in front of an interviewer? Do you make a powerful and effective first impression?
   - How are your smile, your eye contact, and your confidence level?
   - How do you use your body language to your advantage?
2. Assessing auditory performance
   - How is your tone of voice?
   - Are you using fillers (*um, ah, well, uh*)?
   - How is the pitch of your voice?
   - Are you speaking clearly, smoothly, and distinctly?
3. Assessing verbal mastery
   - Are you answering questions clearly, concisely, and powerfully?
   - Are you prepared for difficult or uncomfortable questions?
   - Are you prepared with examples of achievement and accomplishment?
   - Are you primed to ask the interviewer lucid and compelling questions?

By using video training to perfect your communication style and techniques, you will build self-confidence, detect and correct interviewing flaws, and in the end become proficient in building rapport with the interviewer so that you will win the job offer. No one goes out on Broadway before many, many dress rehearsals. The baseball season begins with spring training in preparation for the 162-game schedule. In the same way, you should never enter an interview without your own dress rehearsal or spring training.

Video training, like role playing, is *not* a method that will humiliate or embarrass you. It is just the opposite: a method you use to prepare to perform well. It's better to make a mistake in your living room than in the boardroom, and so becoming comfortable in front of a video camera will help you be more comfortable in front of an interviewer.

Preparing for the Camera

Begin slowly. Take 25 index cards (or as many as you believe would be valuable and necessary) and write down one interview question that you feel you must master on each card. Put all the cards in a big box and set up the video camera on a tripod, or select someone to be your camera operator (family member, friend, or career coach) to film the mock interview.

> The retail cost of video training can be quite high. A great solution is to use a home video camera and tripod. Set it up, mock up the interview, and watch it later. You could even do question by question with the video camera on your phone. It's not great, but it's better than not doing it at all.

Then get dressed for the interview, sit down at a desk just as in role play, and have your partner pick questions at random out of the box. Work on maybe 5 to 10 questions and then stop. Review your performance. Determine where you triumphed and did well. Critique areas where you could improve. Then do this again.

Continue to practice until you are 100 percent comfortable and confident that you are better prepared than the competition is. Remember, the more you practice and perfect your interviewing skills by using video training technologies, the better your chances are of winning the best jobs!

TIPS

If you are shy and extremely uncomfortable, don't worry—we all feel that way at first. Begin the process slowly. Don't spend more than three to five minutes initially filming. Prepare five *easy* questions that you know will be fun to answer. Such questions might follow a scenario like this:

1. What are your name, address, and favorite vegetable?
2. Do you have a favorite number? Why is this your favorite number?
3. What type of automobile do you drive, and do you like it?
4. What is your favorite type of food, and do you have a favorite restaurant?
5. What is your favorite kind of animal and why?

After these easy questions, review your performance and check for posture, smile, and energy level. Most people do well with this and begin to enjoy it. If it is difficult, keep using easy questions until you are comfortable. Once you are fine with these easy questions, you can take it to the next level: easy questions with a couple of challenging (but still not difficult) questions such as the following:

1. What is your occupation, and how long have you been doing it?
2. How did you select this occupation?
3. What are your three to five strengths?
4. What are your weaknesses as you see them?
5. What do you like to do in your spare time?

Once you are comfortable in front of the camera, you can work your way up to more difficult questions. Never move to the next level until you are completely comfortable with the easier questions.

Congruency

Congruency is critical, meaning you can't answer no to an interview question by shaking your head up and down and indicating yes. This may be an exaggeration, but many people are asked questions, and their words don't convey the same response as their body language. Be sure when you are using video technology that your verbal responses (words) are consistent and congruent with your physical response.

Remember, practice makes perfect, and perfect practice results in interview mastery. Use video technology to master your communication skills for the interview, and you'll come out on top almost every time. You want to instill in yourself the following:

- Confidence over doubt.
- Likability over ability (people hire people whom they like and who are like them).
- Proactive preparation rather than a defensive reaction.
- Preparation over procrastination.
- Creativity over conformity.
- More hard work and less whining.
- Achievement over settlement.

CHAPTER

9

Image Is Everything
in Interviewing

ONE OF OUR clients, Patrick, had his first interview with a vice president for the company he applied to at a local restaurant. Patrick arrived early and spent some time doing last-minute prepping while drinking a coffee outside a bookstore. He entered the restaurant five minutes early and waited, and then the vice president, Lisa, walked in about two or three minutes late.

They exchanged pleasantries about the weather and finding the restaurant. The hostess seated them. Then Lisa said, "I love that suit. That is a very sharp outfit." Patrick knew right then that he was in.

Of course, image is not everything, but when you don't know someone, there is little on which to judge except the person's image. If you don't get a chance to know and work with someone, there is not much to go on. This is shallow and may be unfair, but it's often how it is. Most people make up their minds about others within a few minutes of meeting them. Maybe not completely, but the first impression is usually made very quickly. And in many respects, that impression is almost impossible to change. Just as your résumé is sized up in about 20 seconds, so are you. It's not arrogance; it is a matter of image and product.

Does your marketing reflect the image you want? Don't think you aren't doing marketing. You may not advertise or send mailings, but you are marketing every day. People base judgments about your professionalism on your image every day.

When you mail a packet of information, do you simply scribble the name and address on the big mailing envelope? Or do you take the time to type the name and address on a preprinted label? Think of it this way: What's the first thing a potential client will see? The label. Little things count. Image goes to the way you dress as well. My sales team was once selling to Abercrombie and Fitch, which at that time was a casual-dress company. To avoid anyone slipping and wearing casual clothes from The Gap, we outfitted the entire sales team in Abercrombie and Fitch–branded T-shirts. Of course, the opposite is true too. When we presented to GE in New York, "flashy" professional attire was critical.

What is your e-mail address? The real question is whether your address is easy to remember or looks like someone just stirred up the alphabet. Something simple will always catch on, and that's part of the process of image marketing.

Image is a big part of the interview process. Over time you will develop a more personal relationship with your new manager, but in the short run it will be your image that will determine whether you get a chance to develop that long-term relationship.

Dress

Women

Women have much more flexibility and creativity in their wardrobe than men. That is both good and bad. The standard job interviewing attire for women is a conservative dark navy or gray wool-blend skirt suit. Other conservative colors, such as beige and brown, are also acceptable. Avoid wearing a dress. Blouses should be cotton or silk and should be white or another light color. Shoes should be low-heeled.

Makeup should be minimal, with lipstick and nail polish in conservative tones. Panty hose should be flawless (no runs) and conservative in color. You should opt for a briefcase rather than a purse.

Suits

Suits without vests are the best choice for interviewing. Job experts and employers seem split on the notion of pantsuits. Depending on the position, a pantsuit can be acceptable—still a skirt suit is the first choice. A jacket with a blouse and skirt is a possible second choice. Your skirt length should be just below the knee—never far above the knee. The fabric should be wool, rayon, or linen blends; many new polyester blends are great-looking.

The best patterns are conservative: solids, soft plaids, tweed, and houndstooth. Colors are best if they are stylish yet conservative: blue, charcoal, olive green, and dark khaki.

Shoes

Stick to a conservative pump with the heel not too high. Unless you're interviewing at a local dance club, very high heels are out. Flats are out too; find something in the middle. No sandals or strap-backs either. Your shoes should complement your outfit, not draw attention to themselves.

Accessories

First, wear hose. Many women today do not wear hose on the job, especially in the summer. It can get really steamy in the summer months, particularly walking around New York and other East Coast cities. That may be fine on the job, but for interviewing you should wear hose.

Your hose should be natural leg color, avoiding white. White may be acceptable if you wear a white uniform or work in healthcare.

Your hairstyle should be conservative and easy to manage. Today's styles are flatter and straighter than 10 or 20 years ago, but still avoid too much in lift or wavy curls. Wear your hair up if necessary. And please don't play with it during the interview.

Wear some makeup, but go for a natural look—not too much mascara and eye shadow. Also, avoid a bright lipstick. Make sure your makeup is blended, with no hard lines. Wear deodorant and go light on the perfume. If you can smell it, you have too much on. Brush your teeth and use a mouthwash before the meeting.

A couple of years ago I was hiring a marketing coordinator. We had five women and one man come in. The best candidate wore a very fitted suit with a snug top beneath it. It was really too fitted for an interview, and I was concerned it might be distracting in the workplace. We hired her because she was the best candidate, and she was a terrific team member. But her trendy attire almost worked against her.

Men

Your appropriate attire is largely based on your profession. If you are a business professional, a classic suit can't miss. If you are in some disciplines of real estate or retail, a sport coat and coordinated pants can work. If you are in construction or a trade, jeans are acceptable, but khakis are always a better choice. When in doubt, understand what the attire is like where you'll be interviewing and dress to match it or go one notch above that.

Suits

Darker suits are always best, with a lighter shirt. Avoid brown and light gray, silver, and tan. Charcoal, navy blue, and dark olive green are colors that work well. Make sure your suits are wool or wool blends. Wear a lighter-color shirt and a tie that is darker than the shirt. You can wear a shirt that is not white; just make it lighter than the suit color.

A dark sport jacket with gray or khaki slacks always looks good, although less dressy than a suit. A nice casual look is an open shirt (top button open only) with a suit or sport coat and slacks.

Shirts

Of course, white is the most common, followed by blue. Here are two important rules: Wear 100 percent cotton or a blend that is 65 percent cotton or more. If you are wearing a tie with the shirt, do not wear a shirt with a button-down collar; the collar doesn't lie well. If you are not wearing a tie, wear a button-down shirt, oxford style.

A solid color or a light stripe is best. The cuff of the shirt sleeve should extend past the coat sleeve about a half inch above your wrist but definitely not to your knuckles when your arm is extended. Stay away from monograms and use cuff links sparingly. The neck and shoulders should fit appropriately too. If you are not sure, have a clothing salesperson help you.

Tie

No doubt about it, ties are huge. When selecting yours, first make sure it is silk (or looks like silk) and will accept a tight knot. A great-looking tie that does not lie well is not a great-looking tie. The tie should rest at your belt buckle, not higher or lower. Ties are so personal and varied that selecting one is a matter of personal taste. For a traditional interview try to avoid a flashy pattern. If you are interviewing for an advertising or public relations position, something a bit splashier may be appropriate, but as a rule save the statement ties for other occasions.

Other

Shoes must be polished. They cannot be scuffed up at the toe. Your shoes should match your belt, and black is always safest. Socks need to be dark and should match your slacks.

Handkerchiefs are optional but should not be flashy. Suspenders are popular in some parts of the country. They should be attached to the inside buttons on your pants—no clip-ons and no belt.

General grooming is critical in all industries. It shocks me sometimes how people prepare for a meeting. Most do a good job, but sometimes they are just a sight. You must have your teeth brushed and flossed. Don't smoke before an interview. If you must smoke, then chew gum or brush your teeth beforehand. One problem with smoking is that the odor adheres to your clothes. Just don't do it after you shower and dress for the interview.

Take it easy on the cologne. None or a little is better than too much. Keep facial hair neatly trimmed and limit it.

Body Language

When people don't know you, they will use your body language to get a first impression. In many cases the impressions made are wrong, as a positive form of body language may be interpreted as something negative. For example, someone who moves around a lot may be seen as energetic and efficient. In some cases this may be correct, but it can mean that the person is uncomfortable in the situation and also nervous.

Use body language to make yourself appear more confident, powerful, and trusting, depending on what the situation may require. If you give off negative signs, that could keep you from achieving your goal (giving a successful presentation, proposing an idea in a meeting, discussing a task with an employee, etc.).

Also, try to recognize other people's body language, which could mean that they are or aren't interested or that they feel threatened by your presence. In that case you can change your body language to make them feel more at ease.

If you ever get the opportunity to have a presentation videotaped, you may see things you never would have believed.

Your Eyes

Your eyes are the most expressive part of your body. When people talk to you, do they look directly at you or look away? Maintaining eye contact when talking (or listening) to someone gives an impression that you and the other person are confident and honest. Making little eye contact can say that the other person doesn't like you. Making little eye contact can say that you don't like the other person, are shy, or perhaps believe that you are higher in status and think eye contact isn't necessary.

Posture

How many times are kids told to sit up straight and not slump their shoulders? I tell my son that whenever he slouches. You may think of posture as standing tall and upright as much as possible. In fact, it is the natural alignment of your head and body without the use of tension and "locking." Everyone has a different posture, and it usually develops through habit over the years. This may mean slumping your shoulders forward or hanging your head—anything that has come to feel natural.

Your posture may show how you will approach a situation. For example, if you stand with your shoulders hanging, arms folded, and leaning to one side, you will look like you aren't ready for or interested in the task in question. If you stand with strong shoulders, head up, arms out by the side, and closed fists, you will look ready for anything no matter how much stress is involved. Remember, your posture may show how you will approach a situation.

Look at Figure 9-1. The posture on the far right is too relaxed for an interview. And, you see that often. The middle is good, and combining that intermittently with the one on the far left is best. Lean forward every now and then, and sit up straight the rest of the time.

Looking at people's feet when they are sitting may tell you who is an extrovert (outgoing) and who is an introvert (withdrawn). Extroverts tend to have the toes pointing out, whereas introverts have them pointing in.

Those who stand always look more powerful to people who are sitting down. This is the case because they are taking up more space. If you feel comfortable standing, stand so that you look as though you have a higher status than those around you.

When you move around, the space you take up can make others feel threatened by your presence. This is the case because those around you may feel that their presence in the area is less significant. They may move around using as little space as possible. If you are sitting, you can still give an image of power. If standing isn't appropriate, use more space by stretching your legs out or having your arms at the side of the chair. When you are on the phone and need to be assertive, standing up will project your urgency.

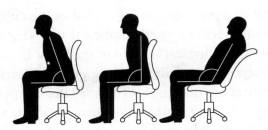

Figure 9-1 Make sure your posture sends the right message

Look out for interviewers who use hand-to-face movements such as holding the chin or scratching the face. This usually shows that they are thinking of you but have some concern.

Gestures

Pay attention to how you express yourself: you might mean one thing, but your gestures could point to an opposite meaning. For example, a simple touch of the nose while you are embellishing an answer could signify to your interviewer that you aren't being truthful.

A lot of us move our heads when we are talking to get approval from others. If you want to look powerful, try to keep your head movements to a minimum.

How much you show your front torso is a way of showing how confident, secure, or trusting you are. The less you cover up your front with folding arms, crossed legs, and raised hands, the more positive the qualities may appear. Folding your arms may look as if you were trying to defend yourself and will make you look bad to the other person.

If you talk to someone who has folded arms and crossed legs and perhaps is turning away slightly, you may think that person is uninterested and feeling detached from your conversation. If people start to unfold their arms and uncross their legs, it may be a sign that they are accepting your issue.

Another gesture to pay attention to is "mirroring." We are attracted to people who are similar to ourselves. Let's say you are meeting with an employee to discuss an issue, and you both take a similar sitting or standing position. The discussion goes well, but if you had taken a different position, it might not have gone as well as it did. Salespeople often sit in a position similar to that of the customer.

A more common gesture is perhaps the one that is most annoying—fidgeting. It removes physical tension in the body. Examples include biting nails, playing with hair, chewing gum, and grinding teeth. Grooming gestures are reassuring. This may involve perfecting your hair or fiddling with your clothes. We normally do this when we are around people we don't know; we groom ourselves to make us look more presentable and lift our confidence.

Interview Image Checklist

	Men	Women
Primary outfit	Wool or wool-blend suit, dark color, subtle or no pattern. Slacks should have 1 to 1.5 breaks in the length.	Suit; wool, rayon, or linen blends; dark or conservative color; pants or skirt. Skirt should be about to knee.
Shirt	Button-down if no tie; no button-down collar if tie. Lighter color than suit; should be all cotton or high-cotton blend.	Simple cut with no frills; may be same color as suit; no cleavage showing. Choose silk or polyester; jewel neck, round neck, or other clean neckline.
Accessories	Belt and shoes should match. Shoes should be dark; black is best; polish shoes; ties should be darker than shirt and not too wild, and fabric must accommodate a good knot. Dark socks, and they must cover your leg when you cross your legs.	Polished shoes; medium heel; should wear skin-tone hose; light makeup, well blended. Nails should be in excellent condition, real or false.
Jewelry	Limit to a watch; nothing exposed.	Subtle earrings, simple necklace, limited or no bracelets.
Hair	Well groomed; clean neck and sideburns; clean-shaven.	Well groomed; not too big or wear up; no doodling with it.
Hygiene	Wear deodorant and antiperspirant; brushed and flossed teeth, mouthwash, no smoking before the interview.	
Eye contact	Give it consistently to build trust. Practice eye contact gestures in the mirror.	
Posture	Stand and sit up straight but not stiff. Lean forward, not away. Do not fold arms across the chest. Try to keep arms and legs uncrossed, though legs crossed are okay. Do not lock ankles.	
Handshake	Firm, in the center of the palm, but not crushing. Squeeze with the middle fingers, not the index finger.	
Gestures	Limit them. No twisting fingers, playing with hair, or anything that might signal discomfort or be distracting.	
Body language	Be confident, somewhat extroverted, perhaps mirroring body language of the interviewer.	
Other	Bring briefcase or leather case with pad of paper.	Favor briefcase over purse.

Finally, our hands are used to emphasize what we say, from pointing and saying "over there" to waving someone away and saying "go away." Hands that are made into a pyramid shape (fingers and thumbs on both hands touching with the palms wide apart) mean power. If someone sitting across a desk from you talks to you with the pyramid gesture pointing to you, this will be your boss or your future boss!

PART 2

DURING THE INTERVIEW

The Five Steps of an Interview

THE FIVE STEPS of an interview are:

1. Preparation
2. Arrival
3. Introduction
4. Rapport building
5. Closing

Preparation

> **TIPS**
>
> 1. Have a day planner or electronic organizer; it shows that you are organized.
> 2. Prepare a manila folder to bring to the meeting. Include in the folder:
>   - Company information (annual reports, sales material, Internet research, etc.).
>   - Extra résumés (6 to 12) and letters of reference.
>   - Ten to fifteen well-thought-out questions for the interviewer.
>   - A blank legal pad, a pen, and anything else you consider helpful.
> 3. Review Chapter 9 ("Image Is Everything in Interviewing").
> 4. Get up two to three hours earlier than usual if you have a morning interview.

5. Eat a good meal a few hours before the meeting to avoid a growling stomach.
6. Call the day before and confirm the appointment. That will set you apart.
7. Be absolutely certain that you have proper directions and the name of the person you should ask for when you arrive.
8. Stake out the company before the meeting. Observe employees going to work. Do they have smiles on their faces? What is their attire? You can tell a lot about an organization by studying employees on their way to work.
9. Do the same thing in the evening. Are there still smiles on the faces of the employees? Do they leave work at 5:01 p.m., 5:20 p.m., or 7:30 p.m.?
10. Practice interview techniques by using video technology. A minimum of 5 hours of video practice, preferably 10, guarantees a stellar performance.

Relax during the drive to the interview. Listen to music that pumps you up. If music does not get you into a power state of mind, think about something that will. Psych yourself up for the meeting. Football players smack heads, crack shoulder pads, and pump themselves up before a game. It enhances their energy level and adds enthusiasm for the event. We're not advocating for smacking someone's head to prepare for the meeting, but you get the idea.

Arrival

TIPS

1. Arrive at the receptionist's desk 10 to 12 minutes before the scheduled meeting.
2. From the moment you step out of the car in the parking lot, consider that you are making an impression on a prospective employer. Show confidence and smile. Use your innate charm and speak clearly and distinctly. Make a strong initial impact.

3. Before meeting the receptionist, visit the restroom to view your appearance. Check your hair, clothing, and general image. Test your smile.

4. As you sit in the waiting room, envision a great interview. Visualize being offered the job. Picture yourself as a contributing member of the company's team. Achieving success is easier once you have it firmly implanted in your mind.

5. Stand while you wait or be prepared to get up quickly to meet the hiring manager when he or she comes out to greet you. You do not want the interviewer looking down at you when you meet. You are an equal participant in this process and want to convey this by standing toe-to-toe with the interviewer. Being looked down on does not accomplish this.

6. Be aware of your body language. When standing and walking, move with poise and power. Offer your hand to receptionist and secretary alike and make sure you have a sturdy handshake. Do not make it bone-crushing, but make sure it is not limp. If seated, sit erect and display confidence.

7. Keep cool under pressure. If you are kept waiting or encounter stress before the meeting, maintain your composure and self-control.

Introduction

TIPS

1. Use a firm handshake, made with a wide-open hand, fingers stretched apart. Grasp the manager's hand and let the manager withdraw his or her hand first. Women should feel comfortable offering a hand, avoiding a limp handshake. A power handshake and a great smile contribute to a great start.

2. Speak in a rich, self-confident manner. Change the tone of your voice as you converse. Speak with energy and conviction. Show emotion.

3. Make direct eye contact. This demonstrates confidence, trust, and power. People are wary about the honesty of someone who cannot make direct eye contact.

4. Determine the interviewer's communication style and adapt to it. Notice how the person walks, uses his or her eyes and body, and dresses. Observe that person's overall mannerisms and behavior. Listen intently to his or her words. Is the interviewer a visual, auditory, or kinesthetic communicator? You need to know this. If he or she breaks into a smile frequently, you should smile often. If he or she does not, avoid grinning.

Rapport Building

TIPS

1. Look for objects that offer insight into the personality and culture of the company and the interviewer as you enter the office. Simple things can be used as an icebreaker.

2. Do not sit until the interviewer is seated.

3. Do not place any items on the interviewer's desk. However, it's okay to do that on a conference room table.

4. Lean forward, with your energy focused toward the interviewer during the meeting. Show enthusiasm and sincere interest.

5. Take notes. You may want to refer to something later in the meeting or when preparing your follow-up letter. If you are uncomfortable with this, ask permission.

6. Use commonalties between you and the interviewer to establish a comfort zone. Light humor and flattery are effective icebreakers.

7. Make good use of openings. For example, if the interviewer begins by saying, "Tell me about yourself," you are in control of an early part of the meeting. Deliver a 30-second personal overview of your background, maybe beginning with education, followed by a 60- to 90-second overview of your career in years (*x number of years doing this and that, working for them and them*). This should accent the

presidential and vice presidential messages (what you can do for the company). There are three advantages to this approach:

- You are able to demonstrate strong communication skills under stressful conditions.
- You are allowed to give a broad sketch of your background and share information to help connect you with the hiring manager, possibly identifying common interests.
- You have the opportunity to summarize your skills and show how they relate to the needs of the company.

8. Prepare for all questions whether you are comfortable answering them or not. The following are a few questions many candidates find troublesome. Rehearse an appropriate answer for each one before the meeting.

- Why are you interested in working here?
- What are your weaknesses? What are your strengths?
- Why should I hire you?
- Don't you think you're too old for this job?
- What qualifies you for this position?
- What was the biggest mistake you ever made, and how did you overcome or deal with it?
- Where do you see yourself in three years? Five years? Ten years?
- Do you think you are overqualified for this position?
- Why did you leave your former employer?

9. Communicate your skills, qualifications, and credentials to the hiring manager when the opportunity arises. Describe your market value and skills, mention how you will benefit the organization, and demonstrate how you will contribute to the bottom line. Communicate to the hiring authority that you can contribute in a meaningful way:

- Save time.
- Improve sales and/or revenues.
- Reduce costs and expenses.
- Improve communications or information flow.
- Solve or take preemptive action to solve organizational problems.

10. Look for hidden meanings in questions. For instance, if you are asked, "Don't you think you might be a bit overqualified for this position?"

the question really is, "Will you cost me too much money?" "Don't you think you might be bored with this job?" or "How soon before you leave for a better-paying job?" Every question has an obvious and hidden meaning. Think fast!

11. Make a good *appearance* and demonstrate *adaptive skills* that show that you have the *ability to perform*—when you do that, you've positioned yourself for hiring.

12. Use concrete examples to illustrate specific accomplishments. *Accomplishments determine hirability.*

13. Call the interviewer by name throughout the meeting. We all like the sound of our names. This works to your advantage as long as you don't overuse the technique. Unless you have been instructed otherwise, use the person's title and last name, *Mr. Smith* or *Mrs. Jones*, rather than Bob or Judy. However, in most cases people will want to be addressed by first name. If they do not, that might raise a flag.

14. Combine good listening skills with hearing skills. Some people listen but do not hear what is being said. Job offers are made to those who listen well and answer questions powerfully and succinctly.

15. Avoid flinching during the meeting. Flinching is an impulse in which the body makes a motion in response to an emotion. People often flinch when asked a question that makes them uncomfortable. As a result, you squirm in your chair, touch your face, breathe heavily, blink, or make movements that demonstrate discomfort. During your practice with video equipment, you should have identified and corrected your flinching habit.

16. Study the hiring manager's movements, and you will be able to determine what is a natural movement and when he or she is uncomfortable with the conversation or the answers you are giving. Hiring managers flinch too! React immediately, adjust your presentation style, and rephrase or qualify your comments. Be sure to react in a smooth and tactful manner.

17. Use silence to your advantage. A few seconds of silence can be effective. Silence gives you the opportunity to deliberate over your answer or qualify a comment. Silence is a highly effective communication technique. H. Anthony Medley, the author of *Sweaty Palms*, says there

are two ways to respond when faced with silence. First, you can wait calmly, remaining focused; the silence may be on purpose so that the interviewer can observe your reaction. The second way is a bit more risky. You can break the silence by asking a question or making a comment. The key is to react naturally, maintaining your composure. Be careful not to talk just to talk; you do not want to offer up empty words to fill the break.

18. Plan, prepare, practice, and rehearse. There is no substitute for preparation.

Closing

TIPS

As the meeting draws to a close, there are usually three issues remaining:

- Salary and compensation package (see Chapter 20).
- Additional questions (see Chapters 16 and 17).
- Next steps (see Chapters 22 and 23).

CHAPTER

11

The Telephone Interview

RECRUITERS, CORPORATE HR screeners, and hiring executives like telephone interviews because they save time and money. They are fact-finding missions. You can slice through more candidates and shorten your list of potential hires through targeted questions on the phone much faster and at far less cost than you can in person. For example, a recruiter can zip through a dozen candidates easily, taking the calls on a speaker phone and writing notes on a grid sheet that will allow a stack ranking of the candidates later. This can be much easier and less pressured than interviewing in person.

The phone interview allows companies to keep everyone at a distance until they are ready to establish relationships with a few select finalists. In a tight job market its use increases dramatically because a high volume of résumés overwhelms companies. Many HR departments have been outsourced or downsized to minimum staffing levels and lack the time to deal with this problem. The phone interview has become another shortcut to the bottom line.

- *Executive recruiters* want to determine as quickly as possible if you are the right candidate. Recruiters sometimes call hundreds of people while conducting a search. They probably will ask a few targeted questions to see if you possess the four or five "must-haves" that place you in their search universe. You may have impeccable credentials and an impressive background, but if you don't have what they want, you may be out.

125

It's a tough concept to grasp. Sometimes it's not that you are not qualified; indeed, you may be overqualified managerially. Sometimes you're just not qualified in the right way.

The phone interview is the first of many "filters" you must pass through. It may be followed by another phone interview. It is not unusual to go through multiple interviews and then subsequent phone interviews with senior management before an offer comes through. Be prepared to have multiple phone conversations with the search firm before being presented to the client.

- *Corporate recruiters* phone-interview potential candidates to save time. While these screeners (or gatekeepers) are not the final decision makers, they can end your candidacy. They may spend more time on the phone with you than will a third-party recruiter because they are corporate insiders and not only will want to check job fit but also will try to assess your cultural fit.

  It is common for executives to solicit feedback on a candidate from their staff. Even the temperature reading that an administrative assistant offers is huge. You need to sell everyone you speak with. When you hang up from a call with a corporate screener, you want the screener to run to the hiring manager and say, "You have to see this person."

- When *hiring managers* conduct phone interviews, they may have a serious interest in you and want to validate an initial instinct before meeting you. A phone interview by one or more of them represents the final check before they bring you in for a day of meetings. They will be seeking assurance that you fit the job and the culture. You need to resonate with them. The phone meeting may even be brief, perhaps while they are waiting for a flight or a rental car. Be prepared for a conversation that may be very focused, specific, and short. It probably will be more pointed than the screening call and will sport more street-smart questions. Expect the conversation to be direct and very real-world.

Phone interviews place the interviewer and the candidate alike at a disadvantage. Unless a job is totally uninteresting to the candidate, most of the decision power to go to the next step belongs to the interviewer, and the burden of selling rests primarily with the candidate. If during a phone interview you feel that an interested hiring manager is unsure about buying you a plane ticket for an in-person interview, you may suggest a videoconference interview as an interim step. Many companies are turning to this method and their own videoconferencing equipment.

If you feel you are a serious candidate for a position, consider offering to pay your own travel and lodging costs for a face-to-face interview. I once did this early in my career. I knew I was the right candidate, and the senior vice president was unsure. I insisted on traveling at my own expense to meet with the people at the company. They were impressed, and I got the position.

TIPS

Here are some telephone tips:

1. *Be up front with the person on the other end of the line.* Feel free to begin the conversation with something like, "I know we are unable to see each other, and this may pose a challenge as we proceed. If I say something that requires clarification or may be misinterpreted, please let me know."

2. *Keep your list at your fingertips.* If you have an interview, you *must* have your list of questions about a company handy, spread out for quick reference. When you are asked about your top three whatever, get excited. You have them spelled out in front of you. Pause and then slowly and naturally reference the bullet points you have scripted out. For this reason, phone interviews should be easy.

3. *Use a cordless phone or headset.* Be sure to ask the person on the other end of the line if he or she can hear you clearly. Then walk around and be animated. Remember, the person on the other end must *feel*

your energy. If you walk and are animated, your energy level will be enhanced, and you'll come across as more vibrant and enthusiastic. Many people have cell phones as their primary phone or only phone. You need to make sure you have excellent cell coverage. A headset on the phone is a great idea, but test it with someone to ensure there is no delay. With cheap headsets there often is a delay or breakup. A cordless landline is your best option if you can, and if it has a good-quality speakerphone, that is good too. That way you can move around a little to muster up energy. Most cheap phones have poor speakerphone microphones, so test that in advance.

4. *Listen and mirror the auditory style of the person on the other phone.* If the interviewer speaks fast, you must also pick up the tempo of your pattern of speech. If the person on the other end of the line is speaking slowly and quietly, you must mirror that style. Listen carefully for choice words and try to use those words as well without overusing them. The key to telephone interviews is to replace the missing "visual" communication style with an effective "auditory" communication style.

5. *Ask questions.* This technique makes sure the person on the other end is fully engaged. Use questions like "Does that make sense?" and "Am I clear, and have I fully answered your question?" and "Can I add anything else that would make this point more concise?" Questions show you care about the person on the phone and keep you from rambling and losing the attention of that person.

6. *Don't interrupt.* The most irritating thing you can do and a sure way to screw up a phone interview is to interrupt the interviewer. Don't interrupt the interviewer or break into a sentence—no matter what. Allow the person to finish, and then you can respond. Be sure to keep a pen and paper handy so that you can write down ideas you want to address without interrupting. Then, when it's your turn to talk, you can bring up the points you want to make without forgetting what you wanted to say.

7. *Keep your résumé available and handy at all times.* Be sure your résumé and a "value points" checklist (messages that communicate your value to a prospective employer) are handy so that you can refer

to them when needed. Be ready to provide examples of achievements and accomplishments with confidence and conviction. If the
interviewer asks a question relating directly to your résumé, you
must have the résumé handy to address the question quickly and
energetically.

8. *Be friendly, upbeat, and positive.* Talk with a smile in your voice and
   change the speed and tempo of your speech pattern so that you
   don't come across as boring. Do not be a monotone communicator;
   that puts people to sleep. Stay positive and have a confident attitude
   throughout. Complete your sentences on the same "high" you began
   with; don't let your words fall off so that they can't be heard. In other
   words, be as energetic at the end of your sentences as you are at the
   beginning.

9. *Dress for success and control* your *venue.* This may sound crazy, but the
   better you dress, even for a phone interview, the better you will
   perform. You will perform differently if you are interviewing in a
   three-piece suit than you will in your underwear. When you are
   interviewing on the phone, dress as though you were in front of
   the interviewer. Also, interview in a venue that inspires you. Again,
   you'll interview better in your office or your library than in your
   kitchen. To be at the top of your interviewing game, you must look
   the part and be in an inspiring venue.

10. *Don't ramble—stay focused.* This is easy to say but not so easy to do.
    When answering questions, be aware of the time it is taking you
    to answer them and stay focused on your primary point. If you are
    asked, "Tell me what your greatest achievement was in your last
    job," keep the answer short and poignant: "I significantly increased
    customer service standards by resolving customers' problems and
    complaints, using my strong problem-solving skills. Would you like
    me to provide some recent examples?" If you go on for 10 minutes
    giving the examples, you'll be rambling and not be engaging the
    interviewer. A good guideline is 30 to 45 seconds in answering the
    average question. Beyond that, you'll want to use technique 5 and
    ask questions while you are responding in depth to questions that
    require longer than 30 to 45 seconds to answer.

11. *Keep your vernacular tight.* Finish your words and articulate them well. There is a difference between pronouncing the word *hoping* and saying *hopin'.* There is a difference between saying "the guys workin' under me" and saying "the employees I was responsible for . . ." Select words with care and consistently work on improving your vocabulary.

12. *Be sincere but not desperate.* Finally, show sincere interest but not desperation. At the end of the conversation ask the interviewer what he or she thinks the next step will be and its approximate time frame. If the phone interview does not lead to a personal meeting, try to analyze the call and look for ways to improve your presentation for the next one. If you lack the right skills mix, there is nothing you can do except move on. Remember that this is not personal and you are faring no worse than many other job candidates.

12

The Videoconference Interview

IF YOU'VE SEEN *The Internship*, that video interview scene is just burned in your memory. The two 40-something internship seekers are crowding into a laptop videoconference with a Google manager in a busy public library, with all sorts of distractions about, with absolutely no experience or knowledge of how the Skype session works. You can find it on YouTube; it's quite entertaining. The short tip is to do everything different than they did in their interview. Having done several dozen video interviews as a hiring manager, we've never experienced what the Google manager experienced interviewing those two embarrassingly inexperienced guys. However, most candidates do have some opportunity to improve overall interviewing skills and specifically their presentation in a video conference interview. And some prep well, manage their environment, and nail it.

Suppose you are asked to participate in a videoconference interview. Our first advice is to try to change it to a face-to-face interview. A videoconference interview will never do any candidate the justice that a face-to-face one will. Imagine all the rehearsals U2 goes through to perfect its craft, only to perform live with a poor sound system. Or a top-rated college shortstop performing his scouting tryout on a poorly maintained Little League field with rocks littered around the field.

It's unlikely you'll have access to perfect video technology for the interview. And if you do, you might not be trained to present yourself through video, like a news anchor is. There are candidates who are "A" interviewers and candidates that are "C" or worse interviewers; everyone's grade goes down in a video interview. You just can't quite get the rapport established or convey the same level of energy through facial expressions and voice inflection. If you can alternatively get a face-to-face interview, push for that. Really do that if it's for a high-in-demand opportunity and you are a close fit.

In practical terms, videoconferencing is a growing medium. It's cheaper than travel and much better than a phone interview, at least from the employer perspective. With the advent of Skype (the most popular amateur use for video communications) and faster Internet connections, video technologies will be more prominent now and in the future.

If you are locked into a videoconference interview, here are some considerations: Know that your interview may be taped by the employer for future reference. No one is expecting you to be a total pro on camera. Still, set your bar high. A couple of hours of prep one time with someone experienced coaching you will give you lasting experience.

Technology Tips

Signal compression for a video interview will usually make candidates less attractive and less energetic. For a Skype interview, you will want at least 1.5 mb up and down, and that is common for most users. What this means is that you want enough bandwidth to handle the video transmission so it's similar to watching someone on television. A low bandwidth will cause the image (you) to stutter and move in delayed frames. Imagine watching television with a DVR and pausing every three seconds. A high bandwidth will be much more like the seamless transmission you see on television. Even so, if you're participating in a video interview, you should look for a facility that could provide you with a good Internet connection and video capabilities, such as a FedEx Kinko's store. You can ask the company with whom you are interviewing to identify a facility. If the company has good resources, its audiovisual or IT team will likely have a network of facilities to call on.

With a couple of days' lead time, test your video equipment. Use the best equipment you can afford, and consider what you can afford. It's crazy and counterintuitive: candidates very often fail to invest in themselves in the job search process. Investing in résumé development, self-branding, and career coaching can pay off in huge multiples. A decent web camera should be used for your video interview. If the one on your laptop is not great, you can buy one for $75–$100 at a local Radio Shack or Best Buy, or you can purchase it online. Make sure it's HD quality with a very good microphone. Get a separate microphone if the quality is not great with what comes packaged.

Then, test it! You must set the bar high for these tests: close to television quality. One other little tip. We mentioned previously that your e-mail address should be neutral and professional; so should your Skype name. Most of the time, it's best to use your name if possible, and if not available, perhaps your name and profession: jayblockrealestate, michaelbetruscoach, or marysmitheducation.

Most candidates are uncomfortable with a videoconference interview. Play that to your advantage. Hiring managers will have lower expectations than in a face-to-face interview. They know it's awkward. By learning and executing these tips, you'll be better prepared than other candidates, and this could very well be a great differentiator for you.

Environment Tips

If the interview is offsite, like at a FedEx Kinko's or a studio, get there early. Call the facility well in advance (not just before) and ask if you can preview the environment. Check out the room, the camera, and microphone. Perform a quick audio and video trial just to see how you come off with the equipment.

Lighting

The light should be in front of you, not behind you. If the camera auto-adjusts to compensate for a light behind you, you may end up a dark silhouette. That's a great fit if you're giving an anonymous interview on *60 Minutes*, not so much for a job interview. Windows should be in front of you or to the side of you. A lamp or desk light in front of you is a great idea.

Sound

A quiet place is a must! Avoid a public place like a library (*The Internship*!) or a coffeehouse. If you interview at home, keep the windows closed, no TV or sound in the background. You'd be surprised what a microphone can pick up—the sound of an outside plane or lawnmower, papers being shuffled, a pet, an ice maker. Not any one thing may be a deal breaker, but it's best to take all those kinds of variables out of the equation.

Clutter

Keep anything within site of the camera free of mess and clutter: papers, pens, books, magazines, background. You're representing yourself as an organized professional; your environment will reflect that, just as your attire does.

Have your notes and company prep organized. One cool thing about a videoconference is you can place notes in front of your computer and they won't be seen. You'll want a stack of 3 × 5 cards, each with a heading for expected question topics and with bullets you will reference. Remember from an earlier chapter on prep, you need to anticipate what will be asked, and you need to be rehearsed on your response. Have a drink of some kind handy, out of camera site and in a neutral cup or glass.

Background

As obvious as this one sounds, you'd be surprised at how many people forget about this. Jay was working with a young client who had a final Skype interview where he was the lead candidate. The position was entry level. The candidate took the interview from his dorm room. Behind him was a poster of a bikini model. The interviewer saw it and was distracted and turned off by this visual, and the young man lost his candidacy. The candidate found out later from a networking connection. Look at your environment and background from the camera point of view: clutter free, no mess, less of everything in the background is better, a neutral wall color. Also, minimize background movement of any kind. No bikini models or offensive posters, paintings, sculptures, or materials that would distract the interviewer from paying attention to you.

Practice the right camera distance and angle so it frames you from the chest up.

Behavioral Tips

Attire

Wear what you would wear to a face-to-face interview. If you wear a dress shirt and slacks, you probably would be fine, but you'll be safer with a suit jacket. Women have more flexibility than men and should follow the guidelines in Chapter 9. For the videoconference, however, avoid a bright-white shirt, as well as stark patterns of stripes or plaids. A solid-color top is best. And for men, a dress shirt with an open collar (one button) and a jacket is better than a shirt and tie without a jacket. Also, wear your outfit all the way to your shoes, not just your upper half. There are some funny stories out there about half dressers who had to get up during the video call and then got caught.

Mannerisms

You have to work harder to project confidence and personality in a videoconference. It's just hard to project a charismatic person in a videoconference. As you practice your answers, do it with a mirror once. Watch yourself. Better yet, tape yourself! Be objective, or ask a friend to critique your video. You want to avoid any jerky movements, expressions, drifting eyes. Sit up straight to slightly forward. Use fluid hand gestures. Nod. Confirm. There will be a perceived connection between posture and confidence and ability. You have to be aware of this. If you're sort of dry and stoic, you'll come on even more that way on video.

Speech

Speak deliberately! Know that there could be minor delays in transmission, so make your sentences short and concise. Slow down your conversation speech by about 30 percent. You have to combine delivering a confident, powerful answer with speaking slow enough to ensure the transmission will make you fluid. You can also make a light comment about this in the interview, to get some feedback on how your audience is receiving your speech. Ask if the reception is smooth and if you are speaking clearly enough for the person on the other end to understand. Inject energy through voice inflection, frequent smiles, and open-eye contact (more about eye contact below).

Side note on slowing your speech: You will notice some people, even at executive levels, speaking fast with a lot of empty words. Generally, you should speak slow enough to let your brain catch up with your mouth and to allow you to deliver voice inflection and energy. Each word and thought should be punctuated.

Eye Contact

Videoconferencing is interesting. With such a limited viewing frame, you'll get more eye contact than usual. In a videoconference, the eye contact is nontraditional. It's natural to look at a person versus a camera. If you look at your screen and the people with whom you're meeting, they will see you looking down, not at them. So in an environment where the interviewer will look more at your eyes than normal, your tendency will be to not look them in the eye (the camera). Crazy! Make a real effort when you're speaking to look into the camera and not your screen. Practice and a role play can get you in this habit.

13

Great Answers to Tough Interview Questions

YOU WALK INTO an interview nearly certain that you'll be asked, "What would you like to be doing five years from now?" The anticipated answer requires a delicate balance of loyalty and ambition. You want to appear satisfied with the current opportunity, but you need to appear ambitious too.

When you answer tough interviewing questions, keep the following principles in mind:

- *Demonstrate your ability to create energy.* A few years ago you could impress an interviewer by talking about using Peter Drucker's management techniques, providing evidence that you knew how to manage. It's different now. In addition to showing that you're a capable leader, you must prove that you know how to encourage individuals to work together to accelerate problem solving. You will have to show you can navigate the corporate culture and solve problems across multiple disciplines.
- *Use real examples from the past.* This is huge. Do not underestimate the power of storytelling. Whenever the interviewer proposes a challenge associated with the position, you need to respond by describing a similar challenge you faced and overcame. Here is an outline you might follow. Remember to be concise, not wordy or boring. Consider the SAR method:

S = situation. Provide recruiters with an overview of the situation. This gives them the appropriate context and helps increase their understanding.

A = action. Describe the action you took in the situation.

R = result. Describe the result or outcome of your actions. Let recruiters know how your actions made a positive contribution to the success of your organization.

- *Show you'll fit in.* You wouldn't be there if the company did not think you were objectively qualified. What really determines whether you'll get the offer is your rapport with the hiring manager, your fit. An interviewer gauges this by listening not only to what is said but also to the way it's said. Be somewhat detailed in storytelling and be articulate. It shows you have credibility and aren't making things up as you go along. Be passionate and excited. Demonstrate that you want to be there and are bright, self-starting, and fun to be with.

Once I met with a principal with Andersen Consulting who was interviewing a Berkeley grad for a position. "He's qualified already," he told me. "I just need to see if he passes the airport test." The airport test? "Yeah. If our flight is ever delayed, can I stand to be alone with him in the airport for a few hours." Get it?

Opening Questions

- *Why don't you tell me a little about yourself?*

  This is one of the first questions you will encounter. It tests your composure, communication skills, and ability to develop rapport with the interviewer. Prepare a 60-second script, "breaking the ice" in the first 30 seconds with an overview of your achievements. The second half should include mention of recent professional and academic accomplishments to enhance your candidacy.

A good template from which to work is as follows:

1. A very brief personal background overview, including your state of origin, academic background, and your current circumstances. A couple of key accomplishments or credentials, depending on the type of position.
2. The most impressive or differentiating strengths that will resonate with the interviewer.

"I grew up in Michigan and went to school at Michigan State University, majoring in accounting. I also played varsity golf and played to a seven handicap. I finished in the top 15 percent of my class at Michigan State.

"Within two years I became a CPA specializing in tax accounting. During my five years with EDS, I have reduced corporate taxes for numerous clients. I was promoted every 18 months or so and was consistently asked back for repeat consulting engagements by Fortune 50 clients. I am currently continuing my education and will receive a master's degree in taxation from MSU at the end of this year."

- **Do you feel you made the right career choice?**

The interviewer understands that many people are not satisfied with their jobs or careers. The intent here is to confirm that the job applicant enjoys his or her profession and that an investment in that candidate will be worthwhile.

"Definitely. I thoroughly enjoy my profession as a graphic artist. Last week I made a small investment in a state-of-the-art software program that will allow me to improve total graphic capability while reducing computer time 15 to 20 percent. This increase in productivity will give me time to handle additional projects and develop new clients. There's no question that I am very happy with my career and see a bright future ahead."

■ *Why are you considering leaving your current position?*

The interviewer is probing for dissatisfaction or discontent. He or she wants to see if you will speak negatively about your employer or supervisor. This question tests your character and ambition. Regardless of the reasons you are seeking a new position, remain positive and don't complain. Demonstrate that you have a vision for your future. Emphasize that your departure will be amicable and professional.

The key message you want to convey is that you are sitting in front of the interviewer and considering leaving because you want to grow. You want more responsibility and growth opportunities.

"My five years with the Coleman Company have been very enjoyable. I was given the opportunity to learn, and I contributed greatly to my department. However, the company was sold, and the takeover has limited my potential for growth. Expansion is not part of the strategic plan for at least three years, so I feel the need to explore other opportunities."

■ *You list four employers in the last six years. To what do you attribute this mobility?*

The hiring process is expensive, and job hoppers are a liability to an organization. However, some individuals are the victims of downsizing. The increase in this method of reducing personnel has affected many competent people simply because they were the last hired or the highest paid. If you are a victim of this phenomenon, tie your answer into these events. If you were the culprit, use tact. You will need to convince the interviewer that you have the staying power and determination to make a career with this company.

Response A

"We seem to live in turbulent times. Having been the newest member on the team with each of the employers listed, I was the first to be

dismissed. I became a casualty of downsizing in spite of my solid record of achievement with each company. You will find that I have impeccable references to support that statement. I am seeking a position where I can contribute over the long term and grow with the company. That's why I am here with you today. Datacom has a reputation of being one of the best local companies to work for in that you retrain employees in order to avoid letting them go."

Response B

"My original intention was to become a systems manager in healthcare, but I haven't been challenged or tested in this capacity during the past five years. As an inexperienced job seeker, I accepted jobs that were not ideal. Now I have set precise goals and know exactly what I want to achieve. I also realize how I can best contribute to a company. This position at Datacom meets the criteria I have set for myself, and I am confident we'd make a great match."

■ *Why do you want this position?*

Desire, commitment, and passion toward one's career goals are vitally important to a hiring manager. Emotion is as important as, if not more important than, qualifications. Confidence comes from knowing your capabilities, desires, and goals. This self-assurance comes across in an interview in your voice and body language in addition to your answers. Confidence is everything! You must know why you want the job.

"I want this position because of the challenges and opportunities Golden Gates, Inc., offers. I have read a number of articles on the company over the past three years, and two of your employees are friends of mine. I waited for the right position to open up and submitted my résumé when the ad appeared. I am well qualified, have a solid, verifiable record of achievement, and have skills and abilities suitable for Golden Gate's corporate culture. I feel the relationship will be mutually beneficial."

■ *What are your short- and long-term career objectives?*

The interviewer wants to see how you envision your future. Evidence supports the fact that high achievers are people who have defined goals for themselves. The interviewer also wants to see how realistic your objectives are and how they mesh with the company's goals.

"My long-term goal is to become an educator in the Bentwood County school system. To that end I am seeking a position as a substitute teacher to help me get my foot in the door for when permanent placement is available. This enables me to prove myself to my superiors and peers and contribute to the educational goals of the school system and the students."

■ *What two or three things are of importance to you in your next job?*

This question is best answered by informing the interviewer that you wish to use your skills and abilities to contribute to the growth and advancement of the organization. That's a safe but powerful response to a fairly general question.

"My total quality management skills can be utilized to improve and maintain high-quality products and services for Marlow Industries and its customers. In addition, I am a team player and would very much like to be a contributing member of a high-caliber manufacturing production firm. I believe that my excellent computer skills can be an asset in a variety of ways, including my knowledge of spreadsheet, forecasting, production analysis, and word processing programs."

■ *Do you consider yourself a creative problem solver?*

This may seem like an easy, straightforward question, but what types of problems does the interviewer want solved? Confidently reply that you have excellent problem-solving skills but keep it general. Specific examples should be given only when the interviewer asks for them.

"Business problems arise in any position. Problems create opportunities. It has been my habit to always present a couple of solutions to a problem we face when discussing it with my boss. I've always felt that if I needed my boss to come up with the solution, he did not need me. For example . . ."

Follow this up with one or two examples of problems you encountered and the ways you solved them. Make sure to keep the examples concise and easy to follow. Here's the thing: Managers like to hire people who provide solutions. Anyone can present a problem or be challenged by a problem. It takes a real pro to present a problem and one or two viable solutions to the manager. That is where this question is going.

■ *What motivates you?*

Answer this question the same way you would answer the question "What's most important to you in your next job?" Inform the interviewer that you wish to use your skills and abilities to contribute to the growth and advancement of the organization. It's a safe but powerful response to a fairly general question.

"As an attorney, I am motivated by challenge, knowing that my education, research skills, communication skills, and experience will be tested with every new case. I am compelled to maintain myself in peak mental and physical condition at all times to provide competent legal advice to my clients. By assisting them to achieve the outcomes they desire, I find myself motivated by our mutual success."

Use this as an opportunity to connect a couple of things that motivate you and are the business objectives you uncovered in your research.

■ *Today we live in an era of constant change. How do you view change and deal effectively with it?*

This is a great question because change is one of the driving forces in our environment. Obviously, you must embrace and adapt well to change. The best way to answer this question is to tell the interviewer that you view change the same way you view problems: as an opportunity to improve things.

"I think change is synonymous with opportunity. Though we all have our comfort zones, I know that change is necessary to maintain a competitive edge and improve our lifestyles. I am highly adaptable to change, learn quickly, and embrace new ideas with enthusiasm and vigor."

- *How do you define leadership, and how would you rate yourself as a leader?*

Understanding the difference between management and leadership is crucial in today's highly competitive job market. Leadership is always in demand and may have nothing to do with managing people. Be sure you know the key differences between leadership and management and emphasize your skills in the right perspective.

"I would define leadership as establishing direction, developing a vision, and aligning people to meet that vision. Leadership is motivating and inspiring others to be the best they can be. Leadership is knowing how and when to initiate change that enables the company to remain competitive and profitable while providing customers with innovative, high-quality products and services. I believe I fit this definition."

- *Would you consider yourself a risk taker or a play-it-safer?*

The ideal answer is to position yourself as a little of each. Interviewers want to know if you are a leader or a follower, creative or unimaginative, a good risk or a loose cannon. It is best to stick to the middle of the road on this one.

"Calculated risk taking is required to succeed in today's highly competitive market. Although I always remain within organizational guidelines and corporate structures, I consider myself a risk taker. I am not, however, reckless or imprudent when I take risks. When I

think about risks, it tends to be to push the limits of our productivity and to get more creative in our problem solving."

■ *How do you make decisions?*

Responsibility necessitates having to make difficult decisions. The interviewer is looking for a system or strategy that you employ in making decisions. Obviously, the company is looking for someone who will make better choices than competing candidates. Be sure to give an example of a decision that was profitable or highly successful.

"First I determine the desired outcome of my decision—what it is I want to achieve. Then I weigh all possible options, do research when necessary, seek out the best advice I can, and assess all the known risks. Once I complete these steps, I make a decision. In this manner I should realize the desired outcome with minimum risk."

■ *How well do you handle stress?*

We live in a stressful society. Being able to deal effectively with stress is important. You don't want to go into depth with your answer, so keep it simple and general.

"A certain degree of stress keeps me at peak-performance levels. Just as an actor experiences stage fright before stepping in front of the audience or a lecturer becomes tongue-tied prior to stepping up to the podium, I overcome nervous, stressful feelings by plunging into a project. Though I do not seek to create stressful situations, when they occur, I use them to my advantage and rise to the occasion. By meeting stress head on, I can overcome it with tact, diplomacy, and professionalism."

■ *What is success to you?*

This is an open-ended, tricky question because the meaning of success is different for everyone. The best answer is one that addresses the achievement of company or organizational goals without compromising any other area of your life.

"Success to me is improving the quality of life for myself and those with whom I come in contact. I feel that success is the result of a continual growing and learning process, and that process enables me to contribute to the growth of the company for which I work. Without growth there can be no success."

Character Questions

■ *If you could begin your career all over again, what would you do differently?*

Unless you are making a career change, the interviewer wants to know that you wouldn't change a thing. You must reinforce the idea that you love your career and, if given the chance, would do the same thing all over again.

"I enjoy what I'm doing now. I was fortunate enough to have a choice of careers, and I chose computer programming. I find it rewarding and constantly challenging due to the strides being made in new technology every day. In order to stay abreast of what is going on, my thirst for knowledge is readily appeased with industry newsletters, magazines, the Internet, classes, etc. I enjoy the constant learning process that the computer industry demands. That's not to say there haven't been bad moments, but no career is perfect. I consider perfection synonymous with boredom. I also enjoy this line of work because I work with people from diversified backgrounds and because every day brings new challenges."

■ *Can you identify three character traits that have made you successful?*

This is a highly subjective question, and although there are no right or wrong answers, there are effective and ineffective ones. Your answer should be brief. It also should be acceptable to all industries.

"Integrity is the character trait that has enhanced my ability to succeed above all others. There can never be any substitute for

honesty and maintaining high ethical standards. I am also passionate
about my work. I love the advertising industry and cannot see myself
working in any other field. Also, I am a lifelong learner, and this
industry affords me constant opportunities to increase my knowl-
edge. I am committed to doing whatever it takes to become the best
in my field."

This is one of those things you should have scripted out already.

- *You have been out of work for over six months. What have you
  done to remain current with our industry's trends?*

This question reflects the concerns of a good many hiring
managers. You should be prepared to address this issue before
the interview, as stumbling here could be your downfall.
Mention how you have improved your skills by taking a self-
improvement course or participating in industry-specific
seminars and workshops. The interviewer wants to be sure that
you have grown and improved while looking for work, not
memorized the soap opera schedules.

"In this highly competitive industry I understand that if I don't
learn something new each day, I am falling behind. During the past
six months I attended three workshops, including one for advanced
spreadsheet applications and a new one offered in this area for presen-
tation task force graphics. I also attended a personal development
seminar, and I am enrolled in an evening course to learn Spanish."

- *What is your greatest weakness?*

Turn this question around and discuss an area that needs
improvement, not an outright weakness. Then you must
demonstrate that you are doing something to improve in that
area. Avoid the overused answers "I work too hard" and "I
expect too much of others." Give one or two examples of
something that will not affect your ability to do the job.

"Everyone has areas in which he or she can improve. Personally, I feel
that mine is in expanding my computer knowledge, both hardware

and software. Today technology is changing so quickly that by the time a person learns a new software program, it becomes obsolete. I am currently looking to expand my capabilities by attending a workshop on doing business on the Internet."

Another good weakness is recognizing a deficient skills set that can be improved. One critical thing to remember is not to give away a character flaw or negative personality trait. Those things can't be changed. Reference a skills set such as training in a certain area, something that can be easily acquired.

■ *What are your greatest strengths?*

This is your opportunity to sell yourself by defining your key marketable skills. Be sure to tailor them toward the specific needs of the organization and the position for which you are interviewing. This should roll off quite naturally, since you scripted it out in advance. The strengths you list should be a combination of your actual strengths and the company's hot buttons you have uncovered.

"My greatest strengths include my ability to focus and see through the clutter [provide a concise example to validate this], motivate a team to success [again accompany this by a concise example], and effectively work across multiple disciplines within a large organization."

■ *Specifically, what is it that makes you seek a position with our company?*

There are only two types of people who can be flattered: men and women. Flattery will get you everywhere if you've done your homework. Be sure you know why you are seeking employment with this company and also make sure that your reasons are flattering to the company.

"Travelco Industries is the uncontested leader in business travel planning and logistics. Your growth has been 20 percent above that of your nearest competitor. Based on my conversations with some of your employees and articles I've read in trade publications, I know

that Travelco prides itself on teamwork and promoting from within whenever possible. I would like to become part of this unique, first-class success story."

■ *Are you a team player, or do you prefer to work independently?*

Teamwork has always been a business buzzword, but you also must be able to work alone. Demonstrate that you can work well in a team environment and produce exceptional results independently.

"I am a team player. Teams win! In today's global market it takes teamwork not only to compete effectively but also to survive. As an integral team member, I work very well independently in pursuit of team goals. I do whatever is best for the company, whether it means working as a team member or independently. I do not have a preference, as I feel each assignment contributes toward the goals of the entire company, which is the ultimate team."

■ *How important is job security in your next position?*

Security in the workplace is basically a thing of the past. You must be secure in the belief that if you continue to add value for your employer by contributing to growth, profits, and organizational goals, you'll have as much security as exists in today's market. Expressing this philosophy in your answer is the best way to respond.

"I know that security in the workplace is basically a thing of the past. I am secure in the belief that as long as I continue to add value for my employer by contributing to growth, profits, and organizational goals, I'll have as much security as exists in today's market."

■ *How do you deal with criticism, and can you describe a time when you were criticized for poor performance?*

This is a tough question to answer. Once again, as with the question dealing with defining your weaknesses, use the word *criticism* to mean areas that could use improvement. Once you admit to needing improvement in an area, you should render an example or two of specific actions you have taken to alleviate this deficiency. Avoid addressing subject matter that would be cause for alarm. These subjects include excessive absenteeism, interpersonal conflicts, skill-level deficiencies, and any other issues that would send up a red flag to the interviewer.

"A person who doesn't make mistakes doesn't really accomplish much. I admit to making mistakes because I am willing to tackle new challenges. I welcome constructive criticism because I learn from it, and I can't recall ever making the same error twice. I recall an example that occurred about four years ago. I was having trouble with efficiently managing my time, and my supervisor brought it to my attention. He suggested a seminar on time management, which I attended later that month. It was an invaluable program, as it taught me efficient ways to manage time at work and at home. I implemented many of the tips from the course and have not experienced that problem again."

■ *How do you get along with your superiors?*

If you got along well with all your former bosses, this question is a piece of cake. If you didn't, be aware that your eye contact, facial expressions, and body language are first to react to the question; your verbal comments are second. Any squirming in your seat or change in expression relays an uncomfortable feeling instantly. Do not bad-mouth or criticize former bosses. Focus your attention on the part of the relationship that was good. If there were no good moments, fake it. Pretend you're on stage, giving the performance of your life.

"I believe in teamwork, and all my former bosses were leaders of the team. I respected them equally, although I liked some better than others. Personal feelings aside, I was fortunate to come away from each position having learned from each of my supervisors. I have always achieved above-average ratings from my managers, and they have sponsored me on more than one occasion for promotional opportunities."

"How Well Have You Done Your Homework?" Questions

■ *What do you know about our company?*

After all the work we did in prior chapters, this should be a no-brainer. Your answer to this question demonstrates to the interviewer whether you have taken the time to research the company and have identified where and how you can contribute.

"HCA Healthcare is the second largest healthcare company in America. You have about 8,000 employees and are concentrated in the Southeast. Last year's revenues were over $3 billion, and you just completed a large hospital chain acquisition in Kansas. This group is chartered to work toward merging the back-office systems of the merged companies. On that understanding, I accomplished a similar transition with ABC Company when we did . . ."

■ *If we make an acceptable employment offer, when will you be able to start?*

This question usually means that there is an urgency to fill the position or that the interviewer is testing your enthusiasm. A high-energy response means you're very interested—a live wire. A low-energy response red-flags you as someone who is lethargic and a hiring risk.

"I owe my current employer the same consideration that I would give you and would not leave without giving a two-week notice. After that period of time, I could begin immediately. I am excited about this opportunity and would not take time off between jobs. I have the enthusiasm and desire to join you without delay."

■ *What do you know about the position we are looking to fill?*

Research is critical. You want to offer more information than is outlined in the advertisement if the position was, in fact, advertised. Your commitment to the research will pay off each and every time. Your lack of research will result in a half-hearted performance.

*"I had the opportunity of meeting with the retiring sales represen-
tative a week ago. She mentioned that Medpro is coming out with
a new drug that will lower blood pressure. That's exciting to me
not only from a sales and profit standpoint but in that the medica-
tion will enhance the quality of life for so many people. She also
mentioned that you would like to target the new surgery centers for
distribution, and I have excellent connections in this area."*

■ *Do you feel that you might be overqualified for this position?*

Being overqualified means that you will be looking for another
job the day you accept this one, will require too much money,
or will be difficult to manage. Overcome these three concerns,
and you'll position yourself to receive the offer.

*"I think it can be a real plus to have someone on your team with
more talent than the job requires. I have set my sights on working
for Artista, and I realize that today's job market requires that we
compromise a little in the beginning in order to advance at a later
date. I know this sacrifice is only short term, as I intend to prove
myself to you and advance as quickly as possible. I assure you that
you will see immediate results from my efforts, and my level of
enthusiasm and energy will be contagious throughout the firm."*

■ *We require a good amount of overtime: late evenings and some
weekends. Will this pose a problem in your personal life?*

Enthusiasm for the job and the ability to be flexible with your
personal schedule are important to your employer. Most
interviewers don't want to hear that you are willing to compromise your family relationships, but they want you to say that
there is some flexibility. In addition, the interviewer is looking
for dependability and reliability.

*"My family supports my career 110 percent. If I have to work on
Saturday, we spend quality time together on Sunday. I am accus-
tomed to working evenings and weekends when necessary. I fully
understand that today's work ethic requires the employee to go the
extra mile in order for the company to prosper and grow."*

- *You have worked for yourself for quite some time, and now you want to work for a company. Can you adjust, and are you not a risk to return to your entrepreneurial ways?*

You must be forceful and convincing when responding to this question because it raises serious concerns to the interviewer. Evidence shows that many entrepreneurs return to being self-employed after a short time with an employer. Companies don't want to hire people seeking an easy paycheck. I recommend an honest, right-from-the-heart answer. Based on the believability factor, you will be either eliminated from or considered for the position.

"Yes, I've worked very hard at my own painting business for the past six years. I was highly successful and developed a great reputation as a boutique marketing agent. However, I confess to being a less-than-average businessman. I did not like the administrative responsibilities connected with owning my own business. I have always enjoyed marketing and advertising, and my work received acclaim from all my customers. I believe I can easily adjust to working for a company because I'll be doing what I really enjoy doing and can leave the paperwork to others. I sold my business a month ago, and I don't plan to begin another."

- *What is the most difficult situation you ever had to face?*

The interviewer is looking to discover what you consider a difficult situation and how you resolved that situation. Again, this answer should roll right out when you are asked. Prepare a good script and spend 80 percent of the time on the solution, only mentioning the problem itself.

"During my tenure with TLP Electronics, I was given the responsibility of dissolving our entire in-house advertising department due to the implementation of severe cost-cutting measures. This required me to eliminate 13 employee positions in addition to my own. After considerable research, I found a company to provide advertising services on an outsource basis. To accommodate this increase in

business, that company hired seven members of my staff. I contracted for outplacement services for the other six and closed the department a month ahead of schedule without compromising the advertising needs of the company. I was able to deal effectively with each employee's emotions and assist him or her in obtaining employment or otherwise planning for the future. I also kept the department functioning until the end and took care of my own emotions and needs at the same time. TLP management was so impressed with the result that it presented me with a lucrative severance package."

- *Can you give me two or three future trends that you envision occurring in our industry?*

  The interviewer is testing your knowledge of the industry as well as your foresight. Be sure to give favorable examples. The best answer will mention trends where your talents are specifically valuable to the company in preparing for the future.

  "In 1960, less than 5 percent of a family's meals were eaten out of the home. Today that number exceeds 45 percent. I believe this trend will continue and level off at around 55 percent. However, people will want to have food prepared for them to take home. I predict that take-out and delivery services will increase. Companies providing these services will grow. I predict that the shift toward healthy eating patterns will continue and that the production of meals without red meat will increase. Over the past five years I have perfected many flavorful recipes for the production of non-red-meat meals adaptable for mass production by a company like yours."

- *What one thing, above all else, do you feel excites people about our product line?*

  The interviewer is testing your preparedness. In addition, she or he is looking to see how knowledgeable you are about the products and to gauge your emotional intensity and enthusiasm for them. A good balance of enthusiasm and intellect will go a long way in answering this question.

  "I have been a home builder for 15 years. When I build a home, I am creating a lifestyle. The one thing, above all else, that attracts me to

FTC Modular Homes is the quality, spaciousness, and affordability of your products. This is reflected in your reputation. It is easy to become enthusiastic about promoting the FTC Modular Homes lifestyle to anyone."

- *Specifically, in what ways will our organization benefit from hiring you?*

This is the name of the game: benefits. You will be hired if you can provide benefits to the company or organization. You must go into the interview with a clear knowledge of your value to the company and the specific benefits it will receive from having you join it.

"My employment at McPherson Enterprises will benefit the company in three ways. First, I am a seasoned fund-raiser and can implement cost-effective programs to raise large amounts of money in a short period of time. Second, I am a motivational-style leader who can rally her troops to accomplish these challenging tasks. And third, I work well within the corporate structure. I interact with the president and members of the board of directors and can enthusiastically implement the mandates that the board sets forth."

Accomplishment-Related Questions

- *Can you give me an account of one or two of your greatest accomplishments?*

The interviewer is looking for a correlation between what you have done in the past and what the interviewer's needs are for the future. If asked for one or two examples, always present the greater number. You'll come across as being more prepared and responsive to the interviewer's needs.

"I sold commercial carpeting for GML Corporation and closed its largest account, a $2.1 million sale. I was competing against five national firms. Our prices were similar, and I had to discover the 'hot button to push' to convince the buyer's people that we should be awarded the bid. I convinced them that we would be able to install

the carpet for a 100,000-square-foot building during working hours with minimal interruption to their employees and was awarded the contract. Just last year I closed a $1.9 million account for GML covering seven states, its first national account."

- *What did you like most about your previous job?*

Your answer should be compatible with the needs of the interviewer. Address the things that you anticipate you will be doing if you are hired. Show enthusiasm and provide specific results that occurred as a result of your actions.

"I enjoyed designing computer systems to enhance operational and marketing efficiencies for Moto Industries. I interviewed members of the sales and marketing department to discover what system they used for tracking leads. It turned out that there really was no system and that the proper follow-up was not being done. This primitive, manual method was losing them money. As programming director, I led my department in the design of a $42,000 system that not only tracked leads but generated key reports that provided other invaluable information to the sales staff. Within six months the system paid for itself by increasing business due to accurate lead generation and follow-up. I know that Travelco prides itself on teamwork. I would like to become part of your unique and first-class success story."

- *Describe one of your failures and how you handled it.*

This can be a tricky question, but a good answer can set you apart from the rest of the field. Treat failure as a learning experience and show that failures lead to greater successes. You must have a good example or illustration prepared for this question.

"I believe that failure should be treated as an opportunity to learn. One incident that immediately comes to mind occurred when my boss was traveling from Atlanta to Palm Springs. He arrived at the airport and discovered that his ticket was out of date. I had changed his reservation with the travel agent, but she forgot to issue the

new ticket and delivered the wrong one. We had done business with the same travel agency for two years, and I never had this happen before. It certainly taught me the value of the saying 'inspect what you expect' even when you think you can rely on others. I learned that I should never assume anything. The travel agency provided us with three complimentary first-class tickets to compensate for its error and straightened out the problem while my boss waited at the airport. As for me, I learned a valuable lesson from the incident."

- *How would your former boss describe you?*

Personalities are not the issue here. Whether you were best friends or not, the key to answering this question effectively is demonstrating your accomplishments. What two or three achievements were you responsible for that your boss would acknowledge?

"As a property manager I have been recognized for effectively managing over 20 properties simultaneously, which is 20 percent more than anyone else in our organization. I am sure he would mention that fact along with my strong organizational skills, attention to detail, and ability to prioritize my tasks. He would tell you that I am a very hands-on leader and that little, if anything, slips through the cracks."

- *How would you go about influencing someone to accept your ideas?*

The name of this game is communication. The interviewer is evaluating the scope of your skills in this area. Listening skills, the ability to understand the whole picture, tact, and persuasiveness must be addressed.

"I know that people communicate in three very basic ways when approached with an idea. One is visual: they must see it in writing. The second is auditory: they must hear it. And the third is kinetic: they must feel good about it or be moved by it before making a decision. I determine which style appeals to my listener and adapt my approach to it. By being a good listener, I am able to discern what the

158 — Great Answers, Great Questions for Your Job Interview

other person is thinking. I then bring about agreement by using logic and persuasion and uncovering a win-win solution for everyone. I have found this to be very effective."

- *Can you relate a time when an important project got way off track and what specific action you took to complete it successfully?*

This question tests your problem-solving skills and composure under pressure. A well-prepared story will showcase your problem-solving skills.

"I directed a team of five people in preparing a major policy manual for an important client; it was an extremely time-sensitive project. We experienced a number of delays in receiving research material and found ourselves four days behind schedule. I persuaded all the team members that we were going on a 24-hour, nonstop schedule and brought in cots and food. During the last week we ran marathon sessions and completed the project on time. The bonus from the quality job performance gave us the opportunity to do phase 2 of that client's project—a $38,000 contract for the company."

- *Relate an instance when you had to make an unpopular decision. How did you deal with it?*

Not all decisions we make can be popular. In fact, many people get paid big bucks just to be unpopular. Select an instance where you made an unpopular decision but it made you a hero in the end.

"As coach of our university's basketball team, I made the decision to bench my star player for poor academic performance. The students were not happy, the administration wasn't pleased, and the press chastised me. Though we struggled for four or five games, the team finally became better able to perform without him, and our hero improved his grades. Before the end of the year, our star player was back in position, and we were in the state finals. The lesson had impacted all team members, as they knew I would bench them if their grades weren't up to standards. That year every player had a GPA of

2.9 or better. The players had won on two levels—as athletes and as students."

■ *What is your most significant personal success?*

Some interviewers see a fine line between personal success and professional success. If you are successful at work but have struggled through six marriages, you may not be viewed as a suitable individual for the position. Try to pick up on the corporate culture and tie your answer to that. If you know the interviewer loves camping and you were a Boy Scout leader, try to use a personal success story related to scouting. Answers about your children, spouse, or personal development or improvement are safe and effective.

"My most significant personal success occurred eight years ago when I quit smoking cigarettes."

■ *Describe the best boss you ever had.*

For this question focus on three things: (1) what you learned from your boss, (2) how you supported the boss's goals and objectives, and (3) how you ironed out differences between you. This shows a good balance and won't pin you down to any one style of management.

"My favorite boss was, ironically, one I didn't like the best but respected the most. She was always offering me opportunities to learn from her, and that's very important to me. I supported her goals and objectives and was able to complement her in areas where she was weak. She never cared for statistical analysis and research, and the development of my abilities in those areas contributed greatly to all our projects. Also, through effective communication we were able to work out the challenges we faced in a professional manner."

■ *How strongly do your references support your work history and related accomplishments?*

Before even distributing your résumé, you must identify and coach your references. I even encourage you to turn your references into testimonials or endorsements. If you don't have strong professional references, you will need to develop strong personal ones.

"My references not only will attest to my skills, qualification, and past achievements but will openly endorse me, I am sure, for this position."

■ *Why should our firm consider you over the many other qualified candidates available?*

The interviewer is testing your confidence level and composure under pressure. He or she is seeking an affirmation from you that you are the best candidate for the job. The interviewer is looking for reinforcement in order to make the right hiring decision. Your job is to provide it.

"I am sure you have interviewed many qualified people for this position. Perhaps they have somewhat similar skills, qualifications, and accomplishments. But I have genuine enthusiasm for the company and the job. I offer you the opportunity to take advantage of my more than 10 years of retail management experience. Most important, I am a person who would professionally represent your company, lead and coach your employees, and attain the challenging goals you have set forth."

■ *How do you think your subordinates view you as a manager or leader?*

The interviewer is probing for leadership skills through your personal introspection. This is an opportunity to reinforce your leadership qualities by backing them with specific examples. I recommend that you use one or two subordinates' references to complement your portfolio of references.

"I am a well-respected leader with a verifiable record of maximizing performance from subordinates. In fact, about nine months ago when a major, complex, and difficult project was completed, my employees

threw a surprise party for me. They knew I had pushed myself to the limit along with them and realized it was the only way the entire team could achieve success. I was very moved. Two of my references are from subordinates."

Try to mention employee satisfaction ratings if you had them and they were good. Offer to let the interviewer speak with your subordinates. Many people can manage up well; it takes much more skill to manage down.

■ *How do you vent your anger or frustration in the face of everyday stresses, problems, and challenges?*

This is a good question because we all have to deal with daily anxiety, and the way we deal with it affects our performance and that of those around us. You want to relate that you are always levelheaded, in control, and solution focused.

"I am very active, exercise regularly, eat well, and practice yoga. I consider these activities to be of vital importance because they give me alternative ways to relieve stress. I can vent my anger and frustration on the racquetball court, while jogging, or through yoga meditation. When I am at work, all my energies are channeled toward solutions. I am always in control, never lose my temper, and always know that there are solutions to every conceivable problem."

■ *To this point, what would you think is your major contribution to your field?*

The interviewer is looking beyond today by testing contributions made in the past to determine what your value might be tomorrow. If you are new to the field, say so, but be prepared to mention a significant contribution you made in another line of work. The answer to this question should be global in scope, going beyond contributions to individual companies and targeting industrywide effects.

"As vice president of the American Society for Industrial Security, I completely revamped the annual convention program. I brought in national speakers and organized cutting-edge breakout sessions,

including a powerful computer workshop. Attendance skyrocketed 325 percent, and I was awarded the President's Star for service above and beyond the call of duty."

Management and Training Questions

- *In your opinion, what makes a successful manager?*

The interviewer is trying to determine your management style and philosophy. The emphasis should be on teamwork, training and development, coaching, and leading by example. A mention of attaining corporate objectives would be appropriate.

"To me a successful manager is one who leads by example and is dedicated to excellence. He or she is a formidable teacher and trainer who challenges employees to be overachievers. A successful manager is a visionary who anticipates, takes action, and is responsible for those actions. He or she is also one who is committed to achieving corporate goals and objectives."

- *How would you rate your communication skills?*

The interviewing process is a communication test. The written test—either your résumé or your application for employment—has already been passed, as the company was sufficiently impressed to invite you for a personal appearance. The interview is the verbal test. Your responses to the questions are evaluated and compared with those of the other candidates. Communication is the essence of almost everything we do when we interact with people, and so a powerful response will go a long way toward getting you hired.

"I work very hard on my eye contact, facial expressions, and body language. I am aware of the quality of my voice and attempt to sound enthusiastic and energetic. I am also very careful in choosing my words and feel I communicate well. I am a good listener and have

excellent public speaking and writing skills. To a large extent, good communication skills have to do with caring about what the other person is saying—good listening skills. Often good listeners are good communicators, and that's what I strive to be."

- **Have you ever terminated an employee, and how did you go about it?**

The interviewer may be assessing your compassion toward others or may have some dirty work in store for the next hire. Also, terminating people creates anxiety and stress for most individuals. The interviewer may simply be assessing your reaction in this instance. In answering this question it is important to show compassion but emphasize the courage to do what is necessary.

"Yes, unfortunately, I have had to terminate an employee. After numerous written warnings, discussions, and attempts to correct subpar performances, I have taken this drastic action. I followed all company procedures and applicable laws. Firing a person is one of the most difficult things I've ever had to do. However, I felt secure in the knowledge that I had made every effort to work with the employee to correct the situation prior to taking this action."

- **How do you rate your time management skills?**

Money can be replaced, but there is no replacement for time. Time management skills are very important. Try to provide the interviewer with a brief but powerful example of your skills in this area.

"I rate my time management skills as excellent yet still in need of improvement. Until I can figure a way to get 25 hours in a day, I'll keep trying to improve. I use an electronic day timer and have a portable phone and a portable fax—all to maximize my accomplishments during the limited hours in a day. I rarely miss a deadline, arrive on time for appointments, and keep my meetings short but substantive."

■ *What types of people do you find it difficult or uncomfortable to work with?*

Be very careful with your answer here. Do not be critical or harsh in your tone of voice. Use a relatively safe example such as the following:

"It takes all kinds of people to make an efficient and successful team. I work well with almost everyone but find some difficulty interacting with those less passionate about their work than I am. I am not saying that it is impossible for me to deal with them, but I become frustrated when I see their potential and they do not. Incompetence is also something I am uncomfortable with, but that is easy to deal with by suggesting additional training for the individual. He or she may want to achieve that potential but may not have had proper instruction to do the job."

■ *How are you at delegating responsibility?*

Overdelegation is bad, and not being able to delegate is worse. Find the proper balance and demonstrate that you do delegate but expect results and accountability from the designee.

"As a manager, a large portion of my job involves delegating responsibility, and I do so consistently. I make sure, however, that the people understand what's expected of them and that they have the tools they need. Then we set deadlines, and I hold the people accountable for producing. I also make myself available if assistance is needed."

■ *You see a peer taking home small company-owned property such as staplers, tape, and pens and pencils. What do you do about it?*

This is a question that makes many people uncomfortable: honesty versus squealing. The interviewer is questioning your values. In a period when integrity is going the way of dinosaurs, your best bet is to confront the issue and defend your values.

"I would approach him and see if there was a reason for taking the items. Perhaps he is working on a project for the boss at home and was instructed to take paper and pencils from the office. Allowing him the benefit of the doubt will enable me to approach him less

critically. If I discovered that he was taking these items for personal use, I would mention that I did not approve and recommend that he return the items immediately. To me there is no substitute for integrity. If he did not abide by my strong requests, I would have no choice but to mention this to a higher authority."

- *What decisions are most difficult for you to make?*

Everyone finds some decisions more difficult than others. However, be careful not to identify a decision that will be an integral part of your daily work. Also, difficult decisions don't have to be difficult; they just need more research or take longer to make, which is an effective way to sidestep the question.

"I have no trouble making decisions when provided with the necessary background or research to do so. I don't consider one kind more difficult than another; however, some take more time to make in order to select the right course of action or the correct solution."

- *What is the most foolish thing you've ever done?*

The interviewer is throwing you a curve and trying to catch you off guard. Do not use a business or professional example. Go as far back in your past as possible and demonstrate that you learned a lesson from it; add some humor if possible.

"About five years ago I took my family on a vacation to a seacoast resort about a three-hour drive from our home. I didn't make reservations because it was the off-season. When we arrived, we discovered it was Harley-Davidson week and everyone on the entire East Coast who owned a Harley was there. There were no hotel rooms available. Needless to say, our vacation was less than perfect. I now make reservations when I want to go to the movies."

- *Is there a time you can think of when you would seriously break company rules and regulations?*

The interviewer is testing your integrity and wants to see your physical reaction to the question more than your actual response. There is one great answer to this question.

"Yes. If someone's life was in physical danger."

Great Answers to Interview Questions for Students

THE MAIN DIFFERENCE between students who are interviewing and seasoned professionals who are interviewing is age and experience. Students and recent grads do not usually have experience, and they are not expected to, so don't worry about that. Your real message is aptitude and leading indicators you can convey that will suggest you will be a good fit. If you can learn to package yourself as a seamless transition from school to work, you'll be fine. Pay particular attention to the prep sections earlier in this book. If you do that and speak professionally with tight language, you'll do great!

■ *What are your long-term ambitions?*

The interviewer wants to see how focused you are and how well thought out your plans are. The interviewer may be trying to calculate whether your goals are compatible with the company's. If you have a dream, state it. If you don't, state a short-term goal and provide generalities for your long-term ones.

"For the immediate future I am looking to find a position with an accounting firm so that I can prepare for the CPA exam. Though I am open to a number of options, I will further assess my long-range goals once I have passed the exam."

■ *Why did you choose this profession?*

Be honest unless you fell into it. In that case be honest anyway, but show you have an abundance of enthusiasm about being a part of that field and are highly motivated to succeed.

"Both my mother and my father are attorneys, as are my three older brothers. I guess you could say I was born to be a lawyer, and I'm sure my family members influenced me. But I made the decision myself and have a career that I thoroughly enjoy. With my desire to specialize in copyright, trademark, and publishing law, I am proving my individuality as the only family member not practicing tax law."

■ *What subjects did you enjoy most, and which did you enjoy least?*

This is a question that may define your strengths and weaknesses; use caution when you respond. Be sure to align the subject you liked most with your profession. For those you liked least, name subjects that have no bearing on your future and will not offend the interviewer.

"As a marketing major, I was delighted with the communications and marketing courses that were offered. I took two years of Spanish that I struggled a bit through, though I finished with a B-plus. Oceanography was a course I really thought I would enjoy, as I love to snorkel and scuba dive, but I discovered that it was a bit too technical for me."

■ *How did you finance your education?*

If you paid for it yourself, admit it; that's a great accomplishment. If you won scholarships or took out student loans, admit it. If your parents or someone else paid your way, admit it with gratitude and pride.

"I was fortunate enough to have parents who could afford four years of college. I did earn my spending money by holding a part-time job all four years. My parents worked hard to give me this advantage, and I made every effort to get good grades to thank them. I hope I can afford to do the same for my children."

■ *What were some of your greatest achievements in college?*

This is an opportunity to toot your own horn and emphasize things you want to highlight. Go for it!

"My greatest achievement was making the dean's list while taking a full course load and working 30 hours a week to support myself. Also, I took an astronomy course where I was completely out of my element. I struggled with it but ended up with a B. It was the hardest grade I ever had to work for, but it was rewarding."

CHAPTER

15

Great Answers to Special Challenge Questions

■ *How do you explain the gaps that appear on your résumé?*

This is always a tough question that must be addressed before the interview. If you have long breaks in employment or a number of gaps over a period of time, you must deliver a brief and credible response. The only way you'll have a chance of getting hired is to convince the interviewer that you will not jump ship with his or her organization.

"My former wife was a top executive for an international fashion company. We lived in 18 different countries over the past 20 years. I wanted her to be happy, so I had to find a job wherever we were living. I saw a lot of the world but was unable to have any continuity of employment. My wife and I are no longer together, and I am now very excited about settling down. I'm looking for roots in my personal life and employment where I can contribute and grow over a long period of time."

■ *Why has it taken so long for you to find work?*

This is a difficult question that must be answered well if you are to have a good chance to land the job. Provide a short, concise account of why you have been out of work, and be sure the interviewer knows that you have been working on yourself and your career while out of a job, not just sitting around.

"I enjoy my profession and always give 100 percent to my employer. I have spent a lot of time doing research in preparation for this job search, and I have had the personal ability to be selective. I have selected Amitec Technologies as my number one choice of employment possibilities. Your reputation is second to none in the state of Florida for my type of work. While preparing for my job search, I have taken a computer course, a time management seminar, and a leadership workshop. I'm very excited to put these into practice and join Amitec."

- *I see you've had many jobs over the last five years. What seems to be the problem?*

The interviewer probably assumes that you are the problem. Today the problem for many job seekers is not job hopping but job chopping and being let go because of downsizing and corporate restructuring. If the problem is job chopping, say so in a forceful and convincing manner. Humor can be employed effectively here.

"I am not a job hopper; I am a victim of job chopping. Although I have had four jobs over the last five years, you will notice that I had only two jobs in the 18 years previous to that. Two of the four latest companies I worked for are out of business. The other two were acquired by larger companies that brought in their own teams. Let me assure you I am a hardworking, conscientious employee. If hired, I will sink my roots right here with this organization and prove myself a real asset."

- *Have you ever been fired?*

If possible, avoid answering this in the affirmative. Use the terms *lay-off, downsizing, restructuring,* and so on. If you were fired for cause and there's no way around it, a safe and often effective route is to be honest, show humility, and take responsibility. The answer that follows is really for a worst-case scenario.

*"I must admit that I made a mistake. I had a 15-year track record
with an impeccable reputation. Our A/C technician was taking a state
exam to become recertified in handling Freon. I scheduled the test for
him, but my workload became hectic and I failed to follow through.
He flunked the test and didn't tell me. So I had an uncertified technician working. We got fined, and I was separated. It was a very difficult
learning experience but a learning experience just the same."*

■ *Why should I hire someone from the outside when I can promote
someone from within the company?*

The interviewer is simply asking why you feel you are qualified
for the job. If it were possible to hire someone from the inside,
he or she would. Obviously, that's not possible. Identify your
key skills and qualifications in relation to the company's needs
and sell yourself.

*"In many instances a team can improve significantly by adding
strength from the outside. A fresh, new look at things often enables
seasoned employees to view projects from a different perspective.
I have eight successful years of reengineering experience to offer
a company. I have the ability to build a powerful team, increase
production, and reduce expenses so that MRB Manufacturing will be
well positioned to meet the global challenges of the new millennium.*

■ *Why do you think you can do this job if you haven't worked for
over 15 years?*

This question is asked often of women who are returning to
the workforce after raising their children. Raising children
is the most demanding job on the face of the earth, and you
need to remind the interviewer of this tactfully.

*"I have worked very hard over the past 15 years. I have stayed up to
date on current business trends and technologies. I am very computer
proficient and work well under stress, can handle emergencies
without becoming flustered, and have excellent organizational skills.
During the 15 years in question, I returned to school and received my
MBA. I may not have been bringing in a formal income, but I was*

working very hard and very successfully. I can do the same for you if given the opportunity."

■ *What do you anticipate to be a negative about working with us?*

This is an easy question to answer but a fatal one if it is answered incorrectly. Every occupation has a boring or tedious aspect. Define it and briefly mention it with a degree of light humor and wit. Treat the negative as an insignificant feature of the job.

"I don't envision any negatives about working for Cocoa Toys. However, since I would be working with more computer technology than in my previous job, I'll have to take extra precautions to back up all my files. Losing data is no fun, and I equate computer crashes with car crashes in that I promise to drive my car and your computer defensively at all times."

■ *Have you always done your best?*

This is a simple but cunning question. Be honest and show how you are consistently striving to improve. We are all human, and humans have occasional letdowns.

"I have always done my best, given the fact that I am human and humans don't always give 100 percent. I am always striving to improve on every aspect of my life. If I am always trying to improve, I feel I am doing my best."

■ *How would you react if I informed you that your interviewing skills are terrible?*

This question tests your response to rejection, fortitude in the face of criticism, and composure. The key is to stay calm, be in control, and watch your physiology. Don't squirm! Remember, failure is failure only when you don't learn something. Learn what it is that you could do better if given a chance.

"I am a professional engineer, not a professional interviewer. If you informed me that my interviewing skills were terrible, I would ask you which parts of the interview I was weak in so that I could

improve for the next one. I am sure you have performed hundreds of interviews. I am just an amateur. However, I am a good student and am interested in your expert advice about how I could improve my presentation skills."

■ *How would you evaluate me as an interviewer?*

Don't tell the truth if the interviewer is terrible! The following answer should work almost every time. Notice how the last part turns the question around and tactfully puts some pressure on the interviewer.

"This has certainly been a challenging interview. I must admit, from my side of the table, I am an amateur at interviewing. Your questions have been well focused, and I hope I have responded well. How do you think I fit the profile of the person you are looking to hire?"

■ *How long do you expect it would take for you to make a significant contribution to our company?*

Assuming you know the answer based on the job description and discussions you had during the interview, go ahead and answer it. If you require more information, ask for it. This is a two-way discussion.

"I would like to contribute immediately but would need more information before I could answer correctly. For example, what are your top priorities at this time, and what projects do you anticipate that I would be working on at first?"

■ *To date, how many other positions have you applied for?*

This is a curiosity question. The only purpose for asking it, other than curiosity, is to give the interviewer a frame of reference for how motivated you are and possibly how close to making a decision about another company you are. Use vague and general terms, not providing an exact number. If you feel you can gain leverage by giving exact numbers and names, do so; if not, refrain from being specific.

"This is one of the first interviews I've scheduled in my job search. I am targeting only a few forward-thinking organizations where my skills might be best utilized. Hudson is my first choice among all the companies I have selected. Do you feel my qualifications meet your criteria for this job?"

- *Do you own or rent your home?*

This question attempts to determine your stability. If you rent, don't be at all defensive. Be honest and brief.

"At this time I rent. I have a long-term lease at Cheery Hill Estates on the Wilson shores."

- *Do you have a valid driver's license?*

This is a simple yes or no question. If the answer is no, indicate that transportation is not, has not been, nor will be an issue.

"No, but I have a number of alternative means of transportation. Over the past five years I have never been late for work, nor have I had any problems coming in early, staying late, or working weekends."

- *If you could change anything in the world with the wave of a wand, what would you change?*

This is an interesting question. Does the interviewer mean anything in the world or anything business related? When you answer, repeat the question in the form of a statement, confirming that your choice is global, not restricted to business. This may be a test to determine what your values are.

"You said anything in the world, so I would have to say that I would alleviate world hunger, especially among children. Children are our most valuable resource in all areas of life, including business."

CHAPTER

16

Great Questions to Ask Screeners and Recruiters

MANY CANDIDATES ARE well prepared for interviews with peers and prospective managers, but sometimes they are less skilled talking with the HR employee who stands between them and the hiring manager. Marketing managers know how to talk to marketing vice presidents. Financial professionals know how to talk to chief financial officers. Not knowing how to converse with the HR screener who's working on the opening can hurt you badly.

Most corporations use screeners to filter out candidates, usually at early stages in the hiring process. They do this to save their senior executives time. And because HR staffs, like those in every other department, are stretched thin, a young, junior HR employee could be making a "go" or "no-go" decision about your résumé right now.

What's worse, you may have to undergo one or more HR interviews before you get to see a hiring manager. It's alarming to think that a person with perhaps two years of business experience is making quick and unilateral decisions about whether a senior-level candidate stays in the candidate pool. This happens all the time.

You've targeted a terrific company and have not been able to penetrate it. The company needs what you have to offer, and you can take that company to the next level. Maybe an old sales foe—the gatekeeper—is stalling you.

The Gatekeeper

In sales we use the term *gatekeeper* to describe the person or group within an organization that prevents us from reaching the decision maker. An example of a gatekeeper in sales might be an administrative assistant or a staff group such as HR or finance. A gatekeeper is anyone who stands between you and the person who might want to hire you. Gatekeepers come in many forms, including receptionists, HR recruiters, and résumé screeners.

There are times when it's appropriate to jump over gatekeepers to gain access to decision makers, especially in sales. An HR or external recruiter is more than a gatekeeper, however. Hiring managers usually trust their recruiters; they don't know the candidate.

Avoid misunderstandings by exercising patience. Of course, it's difficult to be patient when your career is at stake. In most business situations, professionals who can speed up the process are admired. In a job search, trying to speed up the process can trip you up.

There are people whose jobs in part are to keep you from seeing the person controlling the position you want. Sure, they may make you feel as if they're really in control. Perhaps you have heard a reply like this: "We'll put your résumé on file and get back to you if we find a match." The truth is, these people are doing nothing but blocking your gateway to opportunity. You need to figure out how to get past them and contact the decision maker directly. Try these ideas.

Work Through the Functional Groups

You need to find someone who works for the company you're targeting or identify a user group that can give you a chance to meet prospective peers, diplomatically showcase your talent, and keep your skills sharp. Be low key, though. You need to keep your stock high by not making it obvious that you are networking or job seeking. Obvious job searching will turn these folks off. Instead, do some research on the company and then ask a lot of intelligent probing questions. If they think you're good, they'll initiate the discussion about having you join them.

One thing you might try to do is gain sponsorship from someone you meet and ask that person to introduce you. You will be positioned as an internal referral rather than an outside applicant. If you don't know anyone there at a glance, connecting with someone through LinkedIn can help.

Here are some good informational questions you might ask while networking with these people:

- How do you spend your days?
- Why did you begin working at ABC Company?
- What do you like most (and least) about working here?
- How is your product positioned in the industry from an internal perspective?
- Who is running the [one I'm interested in] division? What are the key business drivers and initiatives coming up for this year or next?
- What are the biggest challenges facing your company now (cutting costs, spurring growth, improving margins, finding good people, retaining good people)?

Read the News, Not Just the Job Postings

Terrific information can be gathered by searching the news for business developments, personal promotions, and general company news. Consider looking at the promotions section in the local business journal. You want to be a marketing manager, and a company you're looking at just promoted someone to marketing director. There is a good chance that company has not yet backfilled the position of the person promoted. At a minimum you now have a good contact name.

Call the company listed in the paper, ask to speak to the person who was promoted (by name, of course), offer your congratulations, and give a brief "elevator pitch" describing why you are calling.

The best thing that can happen is that you reach the person you're calling and the manager recognizes your initiative and willingness to research solutions. If your skills match up, you should secure an interview. The worst-case scenario is that you get trapped in voice-mail hell. If that is the case, don't always call from the same number. With caller ID so prevalent, call from different numbers or block your number ID so that you don't appear to be a stalker. I also recommend not leaving voice-mail messages, since they probably won't be returned.

This call should be brief. Your objective is to secure a meeting, nothing more.

Your Screening Interview

You have secured a first interview with HR, a screening interview. The interviewer will usually have boilerplate, prepared questions to ask. A common interviewing model might look like Figure 16-1.

When you do interview with HR or another screener, be prepared to ask questions about the position and the company. Generally, you will be given an opportunity to ask questions near the end

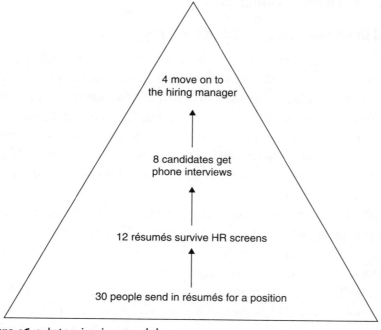

Figure 16-1 Interviewing model

of the interview. You should have at least two or three prepared. If you don't, the employer may think you are not really interested in the company.

Ask questions that demonstrate your knowledge of the company and the industry. Show that you are interested in a long-term career that will be beneficial to both you and the organization.

- Be concise in your answers.
- Answer the questions directly.
- Ask if your answers provided a sufficient explanation.
- Don't overwhelm the interviewer with too much information. Give enough for the person to digest but do not cause him or her to "drink from the fire hose."

Be Nice to Everyone

Don't alienate the HR interviewer by showing frustration or impatience with the process or with the unlucky HR aide who's doing the screening.

Don't treat the interview as a benefits-information meeting and ask the HR interviewer a dozen questions about the dental plan and none about the role. The HR screener is supposed to weed out candidates. As a professional, you need to be as gracious, impressive, and professional in your interactions with HR people as you would be with senior management, or you won't make the cut.

If this seems like obvious advice, why do so many candidates routinely do the following?

- Ask the HR interviewer: "Are you scheduling Mr. Kilpatrick's interviews? Let me give you some dates when I'm available."
- Ask the HR interviewer premature compensation and reporting questions, as if he or she were a wooden post who won't immediately relay such inquiries back to the hiring executive.

- Call the HR employee two days after the interview to inquire impatiently about the status of the candidacy.
- Treat the HR interview as a company preorientation, bringing a list of questions about work attire, travel policies, and local eateries, rather than acknowledging that the HR screener is trying to evaluate the candidate.
- Say something like "I can go over that whole area with Jeff Kilpatrick when I meet him—it's very technical" or something equally condescending.

Treat a Low-Level Manager as You Would Like to Be Treated

It's hard to believe senior-level candidates would make such blunders. Many companies view the way an executive job candidate treats a junior employee when it seems as if nobody is watching as a glimpse of that person's real personality. It can be vital intelligence about the candidate's hierarchical bent or ability to work across levels.

HR professionals are waiting to skewer candidates who fail these unobtrusive personality tests. Don't fall into that trap. Treat every HR interaction the same way you would treat a one-on-one interaction with the person for whom you hope to work. Don't talk down to, berate, or belittle an HR person during the hiring process. Assume that those people know a lot about the business and your prospective role; they probably do. Use your interactions to help them learn more, but not by being preachy. Take the HR employee to lunch if it seems appropriate and isn't overreaching. Return all calls from the HR people promptly and don't treat them as if they were merely administrative assistants (of course, it's worth examining how you treat those employees, too).

Here is an interesting story I was told by an HR recruiter for a Fortune 50 company. When a candidate received a "no thanks" letter, he called the HR manager and was unhappy.

"When we spoke the other day, I had no idea you were screening me!" he said.

"I'm sorry you did not realize that," she replied. "When we discussed this position and your background, what did you think we were doing?"

"I thought you were giving me the courtesy of a preinterview benefits briefing," he said, "the kind of thing that people at my level expect."

"Didn't you realize," she replied, "based on the questions that I asked you, the review of your background, and your accomplishments and approaches, that there was a reason for all that discussion?"

There was silence on his end of the line. "I had no idea you were in a decision-making role," he eventually responded.

And there's the rub. Assume that all the people you talk to at a prospective employer are in a decision-making role because chances are, they are.

Good Questions to Ask

- *What can you tell me about the position?*
- *How many people work for the company or this department?*
- *What type of person are you seeking?*
- *What more can you tell me about the department?*
- *Who is the manager I would be working for, and what is that person's management style?*

See if you can get these questions out early. It will help you frame your answers to later questions so that they are closely aligned with the company's objectives. Assuming this is a phone interview, take some quick notes on what the interviewer says so that you can spin your answers to align them closely with what the company is seeking.

- *May I have a copy of the written job description?*

This is an excellent question. Try to get this out when the interview is set up so that you can prepare in advance how you will make your responses closely aligned with the job description. For example, this will help you script material, as shown in Chapter 1.

- *What would a typical working day be in this position?*
- *How would you describe your company culture?*
- *What is your company's mission statement?*
- *Why is this position open? How long has it been open?*
- *Is this job opening due to growth or replacement? What happened to the previous person in the position (if replacement)?*

These questions are all legitimate. The last four will give you a good idea of what the company is like. They also show that you are concerned about company intangibles, which makes you appear to value the working environment. And they make you appear to be interested in a longer career path with the organization rather than just obtaining a new job.

- *What is the compensation range for this position?*
- *What benefits are provided to your employees?*
- *Do you have a tuition reimbursement plan?*
- *Do you have an employee stock purchase plan?*

Tread lightly with these types of questions. They are good to ask, but you don't want to control the interview with questions that are too far from your credentials. Try to make these incidental questions rather than pre-scripted questions. If you ask about the stock purchase plan, be prepared to discuss at a high level the recent history of the stock. If you ask about tuition reimbursement, have a reason in mind only if going to school connects to overall performance in this position. It doesn't have to, but you may send the wrong message if it is discussed too early.

- *What is the typical career path for this position?*
- *What type of internal and external training do you provide?*
- *How are performance appraisals conducted in your organization?*
- *How are promotions evaluated in your organization?*

These are all good questions that demonstrate that you would be interested in joining for the long run.

- *What is your organization's commitment to diversity?*
- *How diverse is your executive management team?*

Be careful with these two. They are good questions, but you don't want to suggest that you would be a troublemaker or a stickler for a diverse employee base. There are still people making these decisions, and you need to appear as if you would not cause a disruption. In a public company you should be able to determine on your own how diverse the executive team is.

- *What is your retention rate within the company? Within the hiring department?*
- *Has your company had any layoffs in the last two years? What was the criterion for deciding who would be laid off? Do you foresee any additional layoffs in the near future?*

Both of these are good questions. Be careful not to appear scared or insecure when you ask them. However, it is good to convey stability as a critical factor for you in determining where you want to work.

- *What is the candidate pool like? Are there more internal or external candidates?*
- *What is the next step for consideration?*
- *How long does the process typically take?*
- *How soon are you looking to fill the position?*
- *Do you need references?*
- *Have I answered all your questions satisfactorily? Is there anything you would like to know to help you better see the fit between me and your company?*
- *How do you feel my fit would be in your organization?*
- *When will you be making a decision on this position?*

These are good closers. You need to understand what the interview process will be and something about your competition. You also need to understand what the interviewer thinks of you as you prepare to enter the next round. Finally, make sure you've answered all the questions to the interviewer's satisfaction.

Types of Recruiting Agencies

As discussed previously, executive recruiters fall into two major categories: contingency employment agencies and retained search firms. Traditionally, contingency agencies focus on the lower end of the hiring segment, from entry level through middle management. Retained search firms specialize in senior-level professionals and executives. The two types are different in the ways they recruit and charge for their services. See Chapter 4.

In addition to some of the questions discussed earlier, here are some good questions to ask executive recruiters and other third-party agencies:

- *Is your firm retained or filling this on a contingency basis?*
- *How did you find me (if you were recruited)?*
- *How long have you worked with this client? Have you placed for it before?*
- *Do you have a written job description of the position?*
- *How would you coach me to make a good impression on the hiring manager?*

17

Great Questions to Ask Hiring Managers

ASKING QUESTIONS SHOWS that you're interested in the job. It also gives you a chance to show how knowledgeable you are about the position and the industry. Most important, it lets you highlight why you're the perfect candidate.

You have to choose your questions carefully, though, depending on who's doing the interviewing. An excellent question for a recruiter may not be excellent for a hiring manager, and you don't want to ask your potential manager something that's best suited for a future coworker.

Also, there are certain questions you should never ask early in the interview process no matter whom you're meeting. Don't ask about salary, vacation, 401(k) plans, or anything else that might make you seem more interested in the compensation than in the company.

Avoid asking questions to impress the interviewer or asking frivolous questions just to have some to ask. Ask only about what's truly important to you. Avoid asking questions that reveal more about you than about the job. For example, "What is company policy about using the Internet for personal reasons?" has the underlying implication that you might waste time during work hours surfing the Internet and maybe visiting inappropriate sites.

The Hiring Manager

The hiring manager is most likely the person for whom you would be working, although there are instances when you will be hired to work for someone else. Early in my career I was hired by a director for a midlevel position only to find out she was putting me under someone else, a buffer between her and me. It turned out to be a surprise to him, and to me, though it worked out fine.

When you're interviewing with the hiring manager, the most important thing to be evaluated will be personal chemistry. Some might disagree, saying an evaluation of skills is most important.

Nope.

By the time you reach the hiring manager, in most cases, in most midsize to large organizations, your skills already have been identified. The company knows you can do the job in most cases. What the hiring manager wants to know is how you approach work and how you will interact with others in the organization. Maybe he or she will throw out some challenges the company is facing and ask you how it could work through them. On paper the hiring manager has already ranked you on the basis of your résumé and screening interviews.

Your objective is to keep your ranking if you're high or move up if you're not number one. This usually is accomplished by connecting the company's key business drivers to your skills and accomplishments in a likable manner. I frequently coach candidates to ask the hiring manager what the candidate pool looks like and how the people in the pool are ranked in his or her mind. Usually the manager will be very honest about whether you're high on the list or looking like a backup.

The intangibles associated with interviewing, such as rapport building and your executive presentation, are covered elsewhere in this book. What follows are several questions you might ask to impress the hiring manager with your interest in and preparation for the position.

Questions About the Company

External Focus

- Whom do you consider your customers to be?
- What is your value proposition to your customers?
- What is your competitive advantage in the marketplace?
- Are there any industry misconceptions about the company?
- What are the areas in which your competitors are better than your company?
- How does the pressure of Wall Street expectations affect short-term decision making among your managers?

Based on the research we reviewed previously, you should now know much of this. Volunteer the research you have done already. Communicate to the hiring manager that you are interested in finding a position with a winning, stable company that you can help grow in the future. Explain that you are researching the company to make sure this is a good mutual fit for you and the company. Use this opportunity to fill in gaps in your research.

For example, you might say something like this:

"Charles, I read that you are ranked fourth in the industry, but you have the highest operating margin in the industry [something you can learn from Hoovers.com] and the lowest customer churn. How have you accomplished that? Is your goal to end up number one in the industry or to remain smaller but maintain higher margins?"

A question like this does a terrific job of asking a question built on your research.

Internal Focus

- Would you please describe the company's strengths and weaknesses?
- Is there anything you'd change about the company if you could?
- How far out into the future is the organization planning?
- Do you have strategic planning within your organization? How often is it done? Who participates? What is the typical planning time horizon?

These questions are great ways to demonstrate an interest in the organization. They show you care about being part of the company's future. Many candidates interviewing for a position need the position. The company cannot always distinguish those who are really interested from those who just need the new job. Often the candidates are dealing from a position of weakness. If you are dealing from a position of weakness, you may not care about the company; you just need the job. Employers know this. As every sitcom has played out at one time or another in a romance triangle, candidates are more desirable if they are dealing from a position of strength and are not desperate. Asking questions like these shows that you care about what you are getting into and that it's not a one-night stand.

You will also get a sense of how energized the manager is and how plugged in to the organization he or she is. If the manager glosses over the questions, he or she may not know the answers or may not care.

- How would you describe the company culture?
- What can you tell me about the employees who work here?
- Do you offer employee training?
- What is the policy about employees advancing their education?
- How does the company promote and support professional growth?

By probing into the work environment, you will get a sense of the company culture. Listen closely to the manager's responses. Is he a culture champion and energized to be there? Is she enthusiastic about the company? Morale is important. Try to see what the manager is like.

You will also see if the manager appreciates a balance of work and family or personal time or if the work is so intense that it really consumes you (think entry-level consultants or lawyers). It's also a good idea to find out if the company invests in its employees with education programs and training.

- Does upper management have an open-door policy? (*Caution: Make sure you convey respect for the chain of command in an organization.*)
- How are new strategic initiatives communicated to the organization?
- May I see an organizational chart? (*You need to have a good reason.*)
- Is there anyone in your organization who is considered a thought leader in the industry? What is it about that person that makes him or her a thought leader?
- Is the employer truly committed to diversity? Can you give me any specific examples? (*You should have a good reason for asking this.*)
- Do you have an employee stock purchase plan?
- Does the company value training? What are examples of employee development?
- How do you run your initial and future training programs?
- Can you identify typical career paths based on past records?
- Is it company policy to promote from within?

These final questions deal with more generic company policy questions. Limit them. You should have a general idea of some of these answers by now, and you don't want to appear to be focused on the company's benefits. While benefits are very important, they are secondary to the overall position, company culture, salary, and growth opportunities. If you can negotiate a few extra thousand dollars in salary, it will offset any benefit shortcomings you identify.

Questions About the Specific Position

- Which specific skills are necessary to succeed in this job?
- What are the day-to-day duties of this job?
- What does success look like?
- Do you have anything to add to the job description I read on your website?
- What is a typical workday like in this position?
- Are there specific problems or challenges an employee would face in this position?

Try to get these questions in early. The hiring manager is sizing you up on two merits: your personality and your ability to do the job. The sooner you can get information about the job out of the hiring manager, the easier it will be to answer her or his questions with a spin, ensuring that you answer them in a way that matches the way the company wants the job done.

- What do the first 90 days look like?
- Which projects would you like me to complete in the next six months?
- What are the long-term objectives of this job?
- What level of input would I have in determining my objectives and deadlines?
- How much autonomy would I have in making decisions?
- What would be my budget and spending authority and responsibilities?
- How many projects must an employee in this position multitask at once?
- May I ask why the employee in this position is leaving or no longer fits it? Or is this a new position?
- May I seek success tips from the employee who was promoted out of this position?

This is boilerplate. You stimulate the discussion with questions about your duties, current projects, and the like. Take note of the demeanor of the manager. Is the manager congenial or autocratic about your duties and his or her expectations? The last few questions might be a little bold, so use judgment if you want to ask about your predecessor. Asking the previous employee for advice if that employee was not a star performer will not go over well. Also, some employers expect you to hit the ground running; make sure you present yourself as self-sufficient.

These are also good closing questions. Though they are indirect closing questions, they employ the *assumptive close*, a sales term. In theory, asking such questions is an effective (if aggressive) method of bypassing the awkward "Do you want to hire me?" question—in effect you are assuming the manager already has decided to hire you and you are simply asking him or her to clarify that decision. It's okay to assume that the manager will be hiring. Just be careful not to be too presumptuous. Lead the manager there a little; that's all.

- Has anyone ever performed poorly in this position? What did he or she do wrong?
- How do you measure an employee's performance and provide feedback?
- How does an employee know he or she is performing this job to expectations before annual merit reviews?

Getting the hiring manager to explain performance expectations and shortfalls he or she has experienced is terrific. You set the standard for your future relationship. You would be shocked at how often in the future "that discussion we had in our interview" is referenced. Should the hiring manager fall into your "trap" and vent about a previous performance shortfall, you have a terrific opportunity to use examples of your past performance that will support you in outachieving your predecessor.

Questions About Your Prospective Department or the Hiring Manager

- What business problems keep you awake at night? (*This is a fundamental sales question with the purpose of uncovering a key need you can fill.*)
- What are this department's goals, and how do they fit within the company?
- How does this department fit in with the company's five-year plan?
- Is this department responsible for its own profit and loss?
- What is your vision for your department over the next two to three years?
- Does the department face any major challenges?
- Is your department considered a profit center or a cost center? What are the financial expectations for the department?
- Do you have control over your own budget? How is the initial budget amount determined?
- Are budgets made at a centralized location and then rolled down or decentralized and then rolled up?
- Who are the primary constituencies you are responsible for supporting? Shareholders? Customers? Employees? How do you make decisions that conflict with the needs of these different constituencies?

These are typical probing questions to stimulate discussion about the job and the company. They are not high-risk questions.

- Would you please describe your leadership style?
- How do you typically make decisions?
- How long have you been with the organization?
- What has been your career path within the organization?

If the manager gets ruffled by these questions, that will tell you something about his or her management style. This is good information to gather since in reality you work for your boss, not for the company. See Chapter 2 on culture. Your objectives are what he or she gives you, not necessarily part of the big picture. If you like his or her style, say so; state that you have had experience working for someone like that successfully.

- How are you measured as a manager?
- What can I do to make you successful?
- What is your approach with regard to the use of technology?
- What are your organizational values? How do these values influence your decision making?
- Why did you decide to join this company?
- Were your expectations initially met?
- Have your expectations changed over time?
- Do you consider your company to be the ideal employer? If not, why not?
- Do you enjoy working here? Why or why not?
- Have you ever considered leaving the organization? Why have you stayed here so long? What do you like about being here?
- Tell me about a typical working day for you.
- How much travel is involved in your job? (*This might be a little personal.*)
- How many hours a day do you typically work? (*This might be a little personal.*)
- Do you work weekends? How many and how many hours typically? (*This might be a little personal.*)

These are good rapport-building questions to help you learn more about your prospective manager.

- How do you acknowledge outstanding employee performance?
- What major challenges are you currently facing as a manager?
- What are the metrics used to measure whether you are achieving your goals?
- What is your preferred method of communicating with your team?
- What would you consider to be exceptional performance from someone performing in this position in the first 90 days?

I cannot tell you how many managers and individual contributors are surprised when annual reviews are given and they learn new information about themselves and then receive an average performance rating. This is a serious management flaw in business. To be successful, you need to overcommunicate with your boss. You need to understand clearly two things: what measurements make your boss successful and what measurements are expected of you to be successful.

Questions About Your Fit in the Organization

- Who would be my direct reports, and what are they like? May I meet with any of them as an exploratory touchpoint?
- What are my potential coworkers like, and how many are there?
- Can you tell me more about the other people in the organization I would be working with?
- What are the opportunities for advancement in this position? (*However, you don't want to appear as if you were not going to be content doing this job for at least a year.*)
- Why was this new position created?
- Is this a new position, or am I replacing someone?
- What will be the measurements of my success in this position?

Most of these questions are general questions to help you understand your fit in the organization.

"Closing the Interview" Questions

- Is there anything else I should know?
- Is there anything else you'd like to know?
- When can I expect to hear from you again?
- May I follow up with you by phone or e-mail in about a week?
- May I schedule another interview with you?
- What might we discuss in a follow-up interview?
- If you decide to extend an offer, when would you like me to start?
- What's the next step?

The job search and the interview process can be much like sales. Researching company needs, prospecting, and cultivating key relationships are very similar. This is the part when you "go for the close" and try to get the job. After all the interviewing and research, we'll assume you actually want the position. Here you can get the process fleshed out so that you are clear on next steps.

- Is there anything that would prevent you from offering this job to me? (*This is a little bold. Use good judgment when using this one and try to sense if it turns people off. If so, back off and revert to the last question here.*)
- What is your candidate pool like?
- How do I compare with the other candidates you've interviewed so far?
- What is the rest of the interview process? Is there anyone else with whom I need to speak?
- Do you have any concerns? What can I do to alleviate them?

Almost every hiring manager has a pool of candidates who have different strengths and weaknesses. You need to understand the candidate pool. You really need to know how you rank against the other candidates. Most of all, you need to ask directly how the people you have interviewed with feel you would be in the role, and if they are not completely enamored with you, you need to understand why.

In sales we call these objections: they are the reasons the customer (company) will not buy (hire) you. You must uncover the objections that people may have so that you get a chance to address their concerns.

CHAPTER

18

Legal Issues

How DO YOU handle illegal questions asked during an interview? What are illegal questions, and why they are illegal? Laws have been passed to protect individuals seeking jobs from unfair discrimination. Understand your rights and options when you are presented with an interviewing situation that is unlawful. There are six categories of illegal questions based on specific laws that have been passed to protect individuals from discrimination. They are:

1. *Race, color, and national origin* (Civil Rights Act of 1964—expanded in 1968 and 1972)

   Illegal question: Being a black woman, how do you feel you will fit in and work with an almost all-white staff?

2. *Religion* (Civil Rights Act of 1964)

   Illegal question: What religion are you?

3. *Sex, marriage, and pregnancy* (Equal Pay Act of 1963—an addition to the Fair Labor Standards Acts of 1938)

   Illegal question: You seem to be young and of childbearing age. Do you plan on having a baby in the near future?

4. *Age* (Age Discrimination in Employment Act of 1967)

   Illegal question: How old are you, and do you require health benefits?

5. *Affiliations (union initiated)* (Wagner Act of 1935)

   Illegal question: Have you ever been a member of or played a leadership role in a union?

6. *Disability* (Americans with Disabilities Act of 1964)

   Illegal question: Do you have any physical or emotional disabilities that we should know about?

Sometimes interviewers know flat out that they are asking illegal questions or treading on the edge of legality. However, many interviewers simply don't know that some of the questions they are asking are inappropriate or illegal. Although ignorance of the law is no excuse, there is no malice behind the questions, and there is no intent to discriminate. In either situation—whether interviewers are aware or unaware they are asking illegal questions—you must be prepared to respond even if your strategy is not to respond.

Legitimate Reasons to Ask Illegal Questions

There are interviewers who ask illegal or improper questions for legitimate reasons that address real issues and concerns. Yes, they are improper questions, but they are being asked not so much to discriminate as to ensure the right hire. Laws may try to prevent an interviewer from asking inappropriate and discriminatory questions, but if the hiring concerns are real, then even though the questions are illegal, they are genuine in terms of making the right hire. Today hiring costs range between $5,000 and $45,000 per hire. If a company hires the wrong people, it can be costly not only in terms of recruiting and training new employees but also in terms of terminating them.

It is important for you to know your rights, know the law, and then, based on pragmatic and conscious analysis, determine if the question is a legitimate concern of the company and respond accordingly. When an illegal question is posed, you have three options, and each one has consequences, both positive and negative.

Options for Answering Illegal Questions

1. *Avoid answering the question.* By refusing to answer the question or by pointing out to the interviewer that the question is illegal, you run the risk of being right but having no chance to get the job.
   Question: How old are you?
   Answer: I am sorry, sir, but that question is illegal, and I refuse to answer it.

2. *Answer the question in a confident, tactful, and professional manner, knowing there are real concerns in the question being asked.* By answering the question, you have the ability to defuse the situation, knowing that there are legitimate reasons for the question being asked; then you hope for the best.
   Question: How old are you?
   Answer: I am 47 years old, and as a result I bring many years of successful experience that will benefit this company. I am in extraordinary shape, and my energy level is as high as ever.

3. *Walk out of the interview.* Obviously, this is a strategy of last resort. However, once in a great while an interviewer will be so tasteless and rude, insensitive and inconsiderate, that you would in no circumstances want to work for the company, never mind not wanting to answer the question.
   Question: How old are you? We are seeking young people with high energy, and you don't seem to fit this mold at all.
   Answer: Thank you for your time. Obviously, this is a company that does not fit my mold as well. This is an unlawful, not to mention unprofessional, question, and I will terminate this interview at this time.

Within reason, the best tactic is option 2: to answer the question. Try to interpret why the interviewer is asking it and then spin the answer, as in the response to the second question above, so that the potential objection is overcome.

We advise you to keep in mind that interviewing is a method for determining whether a good relationship between employer and prospective employee can be developed over time in a productive and professional working environment. It would benefit most job seekers to make every attempt to answer all interviewing questions as well as they can in a professional manner whether the questions are legal or not (unless they are downright offensive; then one should get up and leave the interview). The objective should be to make every effort to "win the job offer" and then determine if the company is or is not right for you. The goal should be to place the job candidate—you—in the position to accept or decline the job offer.

A Word About Affirmative Action

Companies and organizations may hire on the basis of the affirmative action programs they have in place. Whether you are a candidate who can benefit from such a program or one who might be overlooked as a result of the program may determine the success of the interview. Five groups are protected under affirmative action laws:

- African Americans
- Hispanics
- Asians/Pacific Islanders
- Native Americans
- Women

Our advice is to be aware of these policies. Don't bring them up unless you have a reason to do so and interview your heart out based on your ability to "fit in" and "contribute."

In summary, you must know your rights and the laws as they pertain to illegal questions and affirmative action policies and procedures. You must have a strategy before the interview for how you will address illegal questions if they are asked. You must not bring up or open the doors of opportunity to subject matter you don't want to address or feel uncomfortable dealing with. Most important, do your very best to win the job offer; then, based on your decision-making process, you will be able to say yes or no to the offer.

ILLEGAL QUESTIONS

- *How old are you?*
  Provide an age bracket and answer the question in terms of experience.
  "I'm in my late forties and have an impressive track record of experience and accomplishments in the import-export field."

- *Of what religious faith are you?*
  Answer this in one of two ways. Mention that you practice your faith regularly but do not mix work with religion or, in a tactful manner, state that you do not feel the question is relevant to doing the job.
  "Religion certainly has its place in a great country such as ours. But I prefer to separate religion from work. Don't you?"

- *Do you plan to have children in the foreseeable future?*
  If you don't plan to have children, you of course can answer no. If you do plan to have them and answer yes, you must qualify your answer a bit. Though this is an illegal question, if you refuse to answer it, the interviewer will assume you plan to have children and make the hiring decision accordingly.
  "Yes, I plan to have children in the future, but at this time and for the foreseeable future my focus will be on my career. I feel I have a lot to offer this company and would like to put my skills to work for you. Do you feel that my qualifications meet the criteria for this job?"

- *That's a nice name. Is it Jewish (or Christian or Irish, etc.)?*
  Employers by law cannot ask about your ancestry and base a hiring decision on it. You can avoid the question by saying you don't see what this has to do with the job, or you can answer, "Yes, I am Jewish." Do your best to be diplomatic and tactful.
  "America is a melting pot. That's why we are the greatest country on earth. I feel we are all Americans first and foremost, and to me that's the important issue here. Don't you agree?"

- *Do you have any health problems or chronic conditions of which we should be aware?*

If you have no problems, simply say no. The only instance when you might want to address the situation is if you have a condition that will become apparent in a preemployment physical examination.

"I had a slight heart attack about eight years ago. Since then I have lost 35 pounds, am eating healthier than ever before, and have never felt better in my life. I can provide medical records indicating that I have had no heart problems in the past eight years."

■ *Are you white or African American?*

This is a very illegal question that could be asked during a telephone interview or perhaps in person if you are of both ancestries. Like many of the questions in this chapter, it's extremely unlikely you'll be asked any of these types of questions. This is one question where you might want to go on the offense just a little. There is no excuse for this line of questioning.

"Excuse me, but does this have anything to do with whether I will be considered for the job? I am a person who loves my profession, has a great deal of respect for your company, and would like to be a contributing member. I don't believe my race should be an issue. Is it?"

■ *What does your husband do for a living?*

An interviewer may not ask about your spouse's occupation under the law. Answer it if you wish or tactfully avoid answering it.

"My husband and I keep our professional lives separate. He does his thing, and I do mine, which is to teach. I love the teaching profession and have the skills, abilities, and track record to excel here. Do you feel my qualifications meet your criteria?"

■ *What is your family's economic status?*

An interviewer may not ask for current or past assets, net worth, or anything about your credit rating. The only question an interviewer may ask, and one you'll try to avoid answering, is how much you currently earn.

"Our lifestyle is comfortable, although we're trying to improve it like everyone else. That is why I am here today. Based on what I've seen and heard, I feel confident that my skills and qualifications are a perfect match for this position. What do you think?"

■ *Have you ever been tested for HIV?*

AIDS is a subject of increasing concern for many employers. Today's laws read that an employer cannot ask whether you have any emotional problems, have alcohol or drug challenges or AIDS (HIV), or have received worker's compensation. If you never were tested for it and want to say no, that's okay. If you test positive in a preemployment physical, by law the employer cannot use it to void the hiring offer (unless it impedes your performance or directly endangers other workers).

"No. I have never had a reason to test for HIV, nor do I anticipate a reason to do so."

■ *What is your sexual preference?*

Your sexual preference is of no concern to the interviewer and has no bearing on your ability to do the expected work. Today's laws specify that an employer cannot ask about sexual preference. Though not answering or skirting the issue may seem like an admission of some kind, the best answer is one like the following.

"With all due respect, my sexual preferences, like other personal matters, are personal and private. My personal life in no way hinders my ability to perform the required work. In fact, if anything, family members are highly supportive of my profession."

■ *Have you ever been arrested?*

This is an illegal question, though the most within bounds of any listed in this chapter. The real question you'll be asked, and appropriately so, is if you were ever convicted of a crime. Unless you have been convicted of a crime, your arrest record is none of anybody's business (unless you are applying for a law enforcement or security-type position). If you have not been convicted of a crime, answer no. Any other response will imply yes. If you have been convicted of a criminal offense, be prepared to discuss it.

CHAPTER

19

Win with a Business Plan

THIS BOOK IS worth having for this chapter alone. A key differentiator when you go into a final interview is some documentation of what you have done and can do. When people interview someone they do not know, there is always some skepticism about that person's accomplishments. Everyone needs some validation, including hiring managers.

A client of ours, Patrick, was interviewing for a position as a sales director in a top 10 market with a Fortune 50 company. It was a good position with a compensation plan of over $155,000 plus benefits.

The company had its HR managers screen about 100 applicants (résumés). They narrowed the search to about 10 candidates. Patrick made the first cut. Sandy, the HR manager, called Patrick for a screening telephone interview that lasted about 20 minutes. It was a simple interview. Patrick had the requisite experience and developed a good rapport with Sandy. He was on to the next step.

While Patrick was waiting for a call back, he began researching the company intensely. He spoke with people who worked there and got the inside scoop on what was really going on. He uncovered some of the hot buttons and learned some job requirements from Sandy. He was ready.

He completed his external research on the company and his internal research. Patrick had a good idea of what the company was looking for. He knew he had the right stuff but wanted to show it so that there would be no reason not to hire him.

He began his business plan with what he felt the company needed in the director role and what he would do in that role, and he backed it up with what he had done in the past. It was fail-safe, and he got the job. He completed his business plan in MS PowerPoint, but it can be done in a word processing program too. Figure 19-1 shows what his business plan model looked like.

I.

Document what you think the company needs in this position.

II.

Document what you would do in your first 30, 60, and 90 days.

III.

Back it up with what you have done to validate that you can do what you say.

Figure 19-1 Patrick's business plan model

Figures 19-2 through 19-16 show the 15 slides of Patrick's presentation. He took this deck into his first (and presumably final) interview with the hiring vice president. This is an actual presentation, not something stripped out of industry and discipline jargon. The length and level of detail here is appropriate for presenting a plan to someone with a common background and objective.

The presentation, just like any other business plan, begins with a cover. Figure 19-2 has a simple cover design and simple font, just a basic cover to a PowerPoint presentation.

The agenda, Slide 2 (Figure 19-3), comes next. It is always important to use an agenda or contents slide up front.

Slide 3 (Figure 19-4) is where Section I in Patrick's outline (in Figure 19-1) begins to be addressed. He acknowledges what he believes are some characteristics necessary to succeed in this role. You need to avoid being presumptuous here. If you are wrong in

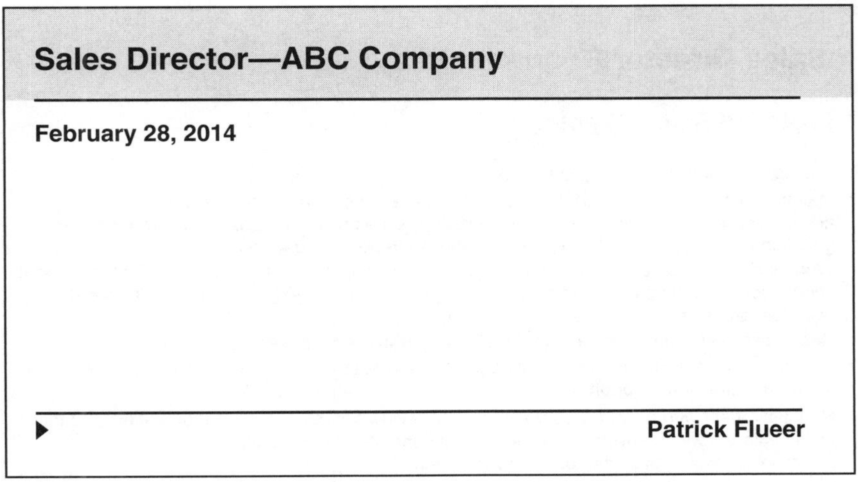

Sales Director—ABC Company

February 28, 2014

▶ **Patrick Flueer**

Figure 19-2 Slide 1

your assertions, it may do you harm. Developing this content takes two things: experience doing the job and an inside track on the requirements for the job. Perhaps the inside track can be garnered from the preceding screening interviews.

Slide 4 (Figure 19-5) addresses what is necessary from the people who would be working for Patrick: subordinates.

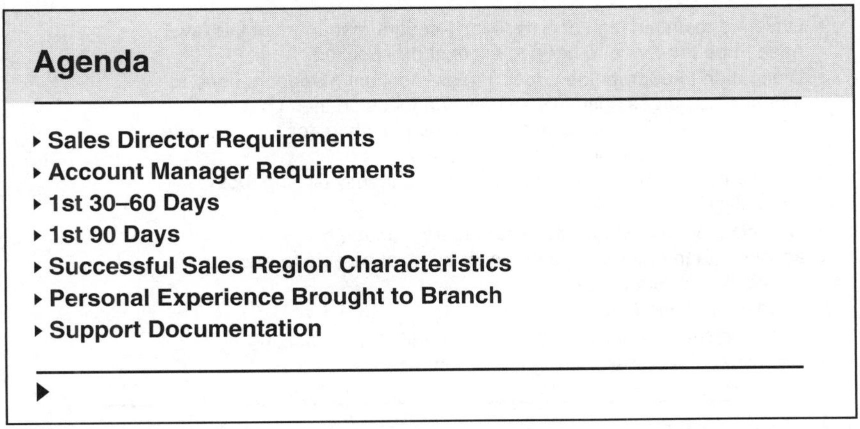

Agenda

- ▶ Sales Director Requirements
- ▶ Account Manager Requirements
- ▶ 1st 30–60 Days
- ▶ 1st 90 Days
- ▶ Successful Sales Region Characteristics
- ▶ Personal Experience Brought to Branch
- ▶ Support Documentation

▶

Figure 19-3 Slide 2

Sales Director Requirements

Profile of Sales Director

- Provide real leadership, not just the title
- Maintain high activity level—need to schedule 50% of time on sales calls with account managers to deliver ongoing mentoring, keep pulse on customer environment, and maintain knowledge of each account manager's strengths and weaknesses
- Work to resolve account manager issues so their obstacles are eliminated; account managers should not waste time on unproductive activities such as worrying about comp, territorial disputes, and similar concerns
- Represent to account managers that the manager works to make them successful
- Engage all support resources, including product management, marketing, PCS, and others, as appropriate for SME support
- Regularly meet with every account manager to review funnel, specific opportunities, and the tactical plan to win the account. Work with account managers in customer communications, both written and "elevator pitch"
- Make sure each funnel has a good balance of different cash values of accounts
- Ensure that territory is fair and balanced in its division and that any account manager issues are resolved
- Ensure larger/strategic accounts are assigned to appropriate account managers

▶

Figure 19-4 Slide 3

Account Manager Requirements

Profile of Account Manager

- Driven to maintain high activity level. Account managers at this level need to be hunters and need to excel at prospecting.
- Delegation to appropriate support roles. Account managers need to manage resources optimally so they can focus on their core responsibilities. Too many account managers shoulder unproductive work versus using their support resources.
- Excellent follow-up. Follow-up skills are frequently lacking, both internally and externally.
- Organization. Growth account managers manage many more accounts than enterprise peers, so they must be able to manage the activity that is required.
- Respect for colleagues and customers.
- Communication skills, both written and oral; key messaging.
- Planning of tactics and timely execution.

▶

Figure 19-5 Slide 4

Slide 5 (Figure 19-6) provides more detail to support ways to manage the group to success. This slide addresses what is needed from the staff to be successful. Admittedly, this kind of information is easier to develop for a sales or sales management position than for a staff position in healthcare, for instance.

Slide 6 (Figure 19-7) begins the second section of the presentation. Patrick has stated what he thinks is necessary for success for the right candidate and the team. Now he is outlining what he may do as soon as he gets in the role.

Slide 7 (Figure 19-8) shows a continuation of what Patrick would do once on the job.

Slide 8 (Figure 19-9) is a continuation of what Patrick would do once on the job.

Slide 9 (Figure 19-10) summarizes the traits found in a successful operation; those traits are transferable to any sales region in this industry and market segment.

Account Manager Activity-Level Metrics

Key Metrics

- Leads: Review best leads and lists; track sales back to leads/lists to build on positive trends
- Prospecting: Desired 8 hours per week, minimum of 4
- Meeting monthly quota: Need to propose twice-monthly quota each week
- Funnel management examples:
  - 2 times monthly quota in 30-day funnel @ 50%+ chance of closing
  - 6 times monthly quota in 60-day funnel @ 35% chance of closing
  - 12 times monthly quota in 90-day funnel @ 25% chance of closing

Figure 19-6 Slide 5

First 30–60 Days

Staffing

- Accelerate hiring for an open head count; time is right for getting ready for 2015
- Make multiple sales calls with each account manager
- Review account manager written communications:
  - Prospecting and introductions
  - Follow-ups
  - Proposals
  - Staying in touch
- Review prospecting "elevator pitch"
- Evaluate activity levels in each account manager funnel
- Understand account manager's strengths and weaknesses
- Communicate to them that one key role of the regional director is to pave the way for their success
- Consider developing account manager mentoring concept

▶

Figure 19-7 Slide 6

First 30–60 Days Continued

Customers/Sales

- Meet with top 3Q14, 4Q14, and 1Q15 sales prospects
- Review account module for each account manager
- Assess tier one, two, and three opportunities
- Assess performers/nonperformers and performance sales plan status
- Organize the approach to the modules from time management perspective
- Conduct mini-strategic account planning sessions for largest opportunities
- Set up joint review on branch with support, engineering for coordination of sales tactics, and key implementations
- Focus on closing best opportunities by making sure we are positioned best

▶

Figure 19-8 Slide 7

First 90 Days

Executive development plan for each account manager

Continue to lead and mentor account managers by:
- Joining them on sales calls
- Helping them on proposals
- Working with each account manager and focusing on closing outstanding opportunities; meeting with prospects and pursuing aggressively
- Helping them strategize on winning accounts by planning their tactics
- Working with them on customer communications, both written and oral
- Eliminating extraneous issues that might be diverting their attention. Resolving any outstanding issues, such as compensation issues, internal struggles, etc.
- Working with them on prospecting activities and improving those skills
- Maintaining very hands-on involvement on account activities
- Earning sales team respect and trust to build their overall likableness and enthusiasm for representing company externally

▶

Figure 19-9 Slide 8

Successful Sales Region Characteristics

It's real execution of the basics—there is no magic bullet. Successful branches, managers, and account managers are the ones that consistently:
- Have very low turnover. Need to hire right the first time.
- Maintain high activity levels. Metrics established must be adhered to.
- Keep group focused and motivated. Need to keep group aware of internal and external developments. More information is better than less.
- Are well disciplined. Branch needs to be tightly managed/supported but with positive and reinforcing spin.

Prospecting and Closing
- Six degrees of separation for account sponsorship—constantly networking.
- Written plan of attack from which to manage.
- Understanding the customer's real motivations; it's not just about "pitching" services.
- Consistent follow-up.
- Asking for the order.

▶

Figure 19-10 Slide 9

Personal Experience Brought to Region

External

- 15 years' experience in telecom industry
- 4 years' sales management experience, with top 25% performance at SBC and #1 performance with BellSouth in 2008 and 2009
- BA in accounting—is valuable when performing financial analysis, evaluating comp statements, etc.

Internal

- 6+ years with ABC Company
- Excellent record of developing strong relationships across many disciplines and markets
- One year of sales management experience managing two sales operations:
  - Number one in direct sales in division
  - Number three in overall market penetration in division
  - Sold largest account in division overall and led in new technological trials such as service for multidwelling-unit buildings and marinas

Figure 19-11 Slide 10

Now, with Slide 10 (Figure 19-11), we begin to get into Patrick's background and why he is the right candidate to attain the objectives set in the previous slides.

Slide 11 (Figure 19-12) begins the third section of the presentation. Patrick has stated what he thinks is necessary to be successful in the role. He has documented what he would do in the role. Finally, he wants to provide some documentation to substantiate that he can do what he has stated is necessary to win.

Charts are always great. Slide 12 (Figure 19-13) quantitatively shows where Patrick's previous sales region was ranked nationally. A top ranking is always powerful, and a chart helps validate him as a top performer

Slide 13 (Figure 19-14) is another chart that validates high performance.

Slide 14 (Figure 19-15) is an extra slide to document how Patrick has managed the activity of his subordinates on a sales account–by–sales

Support Documentation—Prove It

- ▸ Market penetration from sales operation
- ▸ Direct sales statistics
- ▸ Tactical account time management tool
- ▸ Account executive assessments (separate attachment)
- ▸ Account strategy documentation sample (separate attachment)
- ▸ References

▸

Figure 19-12 Slide 11

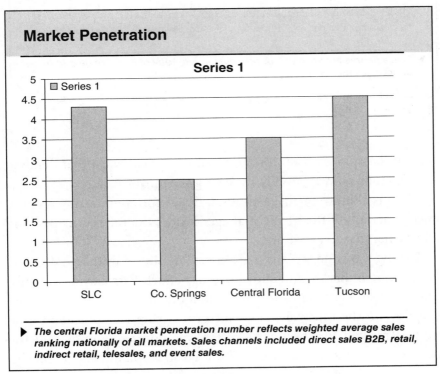

Figure 19-13 Slide 12

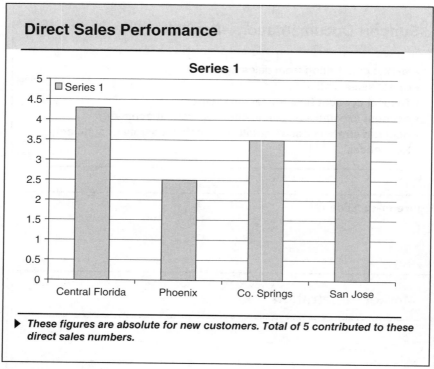

Figure 19-14 Slide 13

account basis. This is optional, but showing real work that demonstrates a high activity level is always a great move.

Slide 15 (Figure 19-16) is optional. We recommend using a reference slide only if the hiring manager knows the references personally. Otherwise, leave it out.

Taking a business plan to an interview shows initiative, knowledge of the industry, and above-average effort. Patrick was the only one of seven candidates to complete a business plan. He went for the close in the interview and asked the hiring vice president how he was ranked for the position. He was number one or tied for number one. Was it because he did a business plan? Maybe, maybe not. Maybe he was the strongest candidate, and the business plan was a by-product of that. Either way, this is a bold way to differentiate yourself.

AE Time Management and Account Planning Approach

	5-Aug	*12-Aug*
All American Semiconductor	▸ Identify both personal references and IPVPN references ▸ Develop account team org. chart to provide to customer ▸ Identify key business partners to leverage for potential references; identify key competitors to see how like businesses are using services ▸ Set up meeting with CIO to meet-n-greet account team to increase comfort level with Sprint competency ▸ Offer up company visit to CIO ▸ Make sure RFP response is getting completed ▸ Create implementation and service plan ▸ Schedule learn meeting to assign action items and schedule two successive calls re: AAS	▸ Second account team call to check on status of RFP response
Banco Santander	▸ Clarify with management—special pricing and no split with NY learn	▸ Present pricing to customer
Blacksone	▸ Implementation meeting on TF services and IP ▸ Follow up on contracts for voice	▸ Follow up on contracts for voice
Crimson Media		▸ Send Danny a KIP email
DelMonte Fresh Produce	▸ Find out about SYSCO Foods and any connection with DelMonte ▸ Find out who new Cisco rep is on account	▸ Contact sales organization to offer up free calling cards for international or conference call cards as a free test drive of collaborative services. ▸ Follow up with Mastec engineer to see if he can help get any sponsorship

Figure 19-15 Slide 14

References

▸ Jane Doe, contact information

▸ Lori Denman, contact information

▸ Paul Garvey, contact information

▸ Judy Heward, contact information

▸ David Hines, contact information

▸

Figure 19-16 Slide 15

> ## TIPS

Here are some brief presentation tips to help you in business plan development:

- Develop a creative template that prints out well in color but is not too busy.
- Align objects perfectly; make sure the pages are well balanced.
- Keep the font size medium (14–18 points). A notorious problem with many presentations is a font size too small for reading or so large it's hard to read on paper. You'd never create a presentation this detailed for an overhead presentation, but in this case you're trying to demonstrate a well-thought-out plan.
- Appearance counts! If you are pushing an artistic or imaginative idea, show some creativity (but without compromising ease of reading and without deleting facts).
- Use informative headings in the document. Use lots of subtitles and let them sell your idea. Think of *USA Today*: short paragraphs and headlines that convey information even if you don't read the article. Make it easy for readers to find what they want to know.
- Use the five Ws. Good marketers tell who, what, where, when, and why, along with how, in their articles. Be sure your interview plan does the same thing.
- Keep it short. No matter how complex your technology or how abstract your concept, you need to get all the information the interviewer needs into 6 to 15 slides or an equivalent number of pages (fewer pages than slides, remember).
- Package it nicely. Use charts, tables, graphics, or illustrations to break up long passages of words. Add a spot of color on the pages if you have the option—a colored line on the pages or a colored logo or other "spot" color. Readability studies say that adding a second color increases retention of information.
- If you use the company logo in the presentation, be careful not to "violate" brand or marketing restrictions.
- Try putting the major point of the slide in a short sentence or caption. That helps the interviewer understand your point.
- Make sure there are no typos. Proof it and spell-check it.

PART 3

AFTER THE INTERVIEW

Salary Negotiation

"THAT'S FINE."

You know what? Those two words may have cost you a bunch! Maybe they:

- Cost you the new Lexus you were hoping for.
- Prevented your kids from going to that private school or, worse, college.
- Flushed that new bedroom set down the tubes.
- Screwed up your retirement savings for the next couple of years.
- Yanked your kid out of college because you were $25,000 short.

Why does this happen? Because negotiating is hard. It's easier just to say yes. Karrass Negotiating Seminars make a fortune because negotiating is tough.

I once hired a sales coordinator for a new office. We were a Fortune 50 company opening up a new office in Melbourne, Florida. Our HR guidelines were between $32,000 and $46,000, a large spread.

The process began with candidates submitting résumés to a post office box in the Midwest. Our HR department screened them and gave me about eight résumés. I narrowed it down to four based on the companies the women worked for, the appearance of their résumés, and their time in the market. I was new to the area and wanted a staff that knew the market.

Three of the four candidates said that they earned in the middle to high $20,000s. I knew this was a small market, but I perceived them to be of less value than the fourth, who did not disclose her salary. I hired the fourth one, who was earning about $32,000 a year. I bumped her up to $37,000, and she was more loyal, energetic, and hardworking than the guy who ended up being her direct manager, who was earning twice that. If you're at minimum wage and the hiring manager says "$9 an hour," a "that's fine" response will freeze it right there. However, a hesitant-pause response could increase it, and another dollar an hour more will earn you more than $1,500 in a year. There's one month of rent in a nice place or a handful of car payments.

The same goes for all other levels too. A simple pause and follow-up inquiry can change a salary by 2 to 10 percent, sometimes more. At professional levels many hires are brought in at 90 percent of the midpoint. That is desirable from an HR perspective because it keeps you in the range and gives you room to get increases without going out of the range. This also means there is a little wiggle room.

The biggest fear in negotiating a salary is that the manager will change his or her mind. In most cases the manager won't and will be impressed by your negotiating and valuing yourself. It shows you're taking the position seriously. If the company chooses the next candidate or goes through the whole recruiting-interviewing-hiring process again, it will cost much more than a few thousand (depending on the level) in the long run. I bet you will get at least a little more.

Negotiating Tactics

Easier said than done, huh? We've all been there. I know I left money on the table early in my career because I wanted whatever the company would give me. In another case I did not counter because the position was such a step up that it didn't matter.

How do you begin countering? First, repeat the offer before going into the "contemplative" routine. You're acting as if you're disappointed or contemplating, but inside you're elated that you've come this far.

In a sales training seminar we were posed this scenario: Suppose you're selling a car. The buyer asks, "How much do you want for the car?" You say "$10,000." If he says "Sold!" right away, how do you feel? What is your first thought? That's right! You think, "Darn it! He agreed so quickly, I guess I was too low. I could have gotten more!"

Now notice what happens if the buyer pauses and says, "Well, is that the best you can do?" You reply, "Yes. I've done my homework, and this is a fair deal on this car; it's the best I can do." When you wrap it up, you receive the $10,000 asking price. Moreover, you also get the inner satisfaction of winning in the negotiation by sticking to your guns.

Does this relate to salary negotiation? A little. Your future employer probably will not bicker as much as bump up a little and hold. However, in one salary negotiation the hiring manager did do what the seller above did. It was an internal promotion I was going for, and when offered the job, I tried to leverage a larger increase. At the time it was company policy to increase a salary only 5 percent per grade level. That amount would have put me well below the midpoint.

Once the hiring vice president indicated that he wanted me, I initiated the salary discussion. I commented that I was aware of the policy mentioned above. He agreed. He thought the offer was fixed and a done deal. I told him my present salary and said that I was already at the midpoint in my current position. That would have put me well at the bottom of the salaries among my peers. I then offered him an informal comparison of me and those peers and said that I needed to stay motivated. I said it jokingly so that it would not come off as negative or get the offer rescinded.

He was empathetic and got me another $7,000 in base salary.

Self-Funding

The following case study still amazes me. I was helping a dental hygienist negotiate a higher compensation for a role she'd been in for over a year. The dental hygienist liked her job and was earning

$35 an hour (in 2014). She felt that was a little below market value but really liked the practice. So how could she get a raise?

She created a one-page sheet for her dentist showing how she could increase revenue with a multiple of 3:1 to increase her wage by $10 an hour. She showed how she could add three fluoride treatments a week and two crowns and would generate much more by really better serving the patients. The meeting with her boss lasted all of 15 minutes, and she got her raise. Now, she'll have to deliver on that contribution. As of this writing, it's playing out just how she proposed.

This is what I refer to as self-funding: the idea is to present a plan where you get a higher salary based on contribution and where the increase does not cost the company any more. Your productivity contribution "self-funds" your higher salary. This is a great tactic for current employees and candidates. You need to know your market value and your ability to contribute. To pull this off, you will have to have a real expertise in your discipline, in a way that you have complete credibility with whom you are negotiating. It's also much easier in revenue-generating roles followed by cost-saving roles. Be creative. How many dental hygienists consider themselves revenue generators? With some creative thought, many, many positions can be spun as revenue generators or cost savers.

Prepare, as Always

Salaries depend mainly on two things: the actual work and the geographic area, related to cost of living. Many large companies in like industries share salary data with one another. A typical Fortune 500 HR department will have a salary distribution breakdown for each position and each geographic region. The HR folks generally know within a pretty narrow range what your job is worth.

Before you begin negotiating, you must have a minimum salary figure in mind. If possible, you should talk to several people who are doing similar work in an area with similar living costs. Watch out! People from Tampa, for example, have no idea how expensive it is to live in the Bay Area or even Denver. You very often get a more favorable relationship between salary and cost of living in less expensive markets such as Dallas and Atlanta than in Chicago, New York, and southern California. You may earn less, but not so much less in light of the less expensive housing and taxes.

Have a minimum figure in your head but *don't reveal it*. The purpose of the method is to get the company to be the first party to name a number. If it's above your minimum, you accept. If it's too low, you say it's too low, but you *do not say by how much*. The person will either break off negotiations or come back with a higher offer. Your only response is "okay" or "higher." However, again, avoid saying how much higher.

Their Side

When you interview, the hiring manager and HR manager want to hire you. The easiest thing for them is to move beyond the hiring process and get back to work. Hiring is costly and time-consuming. The first four stages of the interview have enabled you to develop a solid relationship with the facilitator. You have promoted yourself as the best candidate for the job. It is getting near the end of the interview, and then comes the question "What type of salary are you expecting to receive if selected for this position?" or "What was your salary in your last position?"

Unless you are applying for a volunteer position, you expect payment. It is also a pretty safe bet that the employer expects to pay you. Therefore, you are beginning the process with an unspoken point of agreement. Why does the subject of *how much salary* make both sides a little squeamish? It should not create a problem for you if you have researched the equitable salary for the position.

Work It Up

When preparing for salary discussions, an important analytical form to use is the Compensation Model. This model offers you a visual representation of the three operating principles for compensation negotiation. Knowledge of these three ranges gives you powerful information for salary discussions with a potential employer.

The Compensation Model

Description	Range	Amount
The salary range for similar positions in your geographic area	Geographic	$ _____
The salary range for the position(s) you are seeking with this company	Company specific	$ _____
Your personal requirements	Personal requirements	$ _____

To discuss the issue of salary effectively, you must identify all three financial ranges and expect to operate within those parameters. Obviously, your personal range must be in line with the other two, or you can expect to encounter some challenges.

There are many ways to find out what the going salary is for a position. The following websites offer some information: Datamasters.com, Bestplaces.net, and homefair.com. If you did a simple Google search on "salary comparisons," you probably would get linked to many other sources.

Example

Paulina is seeking a position as a marketing manager for a large corporation. She did her homework and concluded the following:

The Compensation Model

Description	Range	Amount
The salary range for similar positions in your geographic area	Geographic	Between $56,000 and $103,000

The Compensation Model (*continued*)

Description	Range	Amount
The salary range for the position(s) you are seeking with this company	Company specific	Between $68,000 and $89,000
Your personal requirements	Personal requirements	Low of $65,000 but would like to start at $80,000

Based on her perceived value to the company, Paulina is now able to discuss salary comfortably because she has all the data needed to specify her economic needs.

When should you discuss salary and compensation packages? Although there are two options regarding the time to negotiate, your hand may be forced by the interviewer. However, you should attempt either of the following:

- Hold out as long as possible. The best time to discuss salary is *after the offer but before acceptance.* Challenge the employer to divulge his or her salary figures first.
- Go with the flow and discuss it whenever the subject is raised or the opportunity presents itself.

Holdout Example 1

Employer: *"Mr. Smith, what salary are you seeking?"*

Candidate: *"Well, Mr. Jones, there are two reasons why I'm here today. I would be foolish to deny that money is very important, but financial considerations are secondary to securing the right job with the right company. I'm more interested in challenge and opportunity. So far I am very impressed with what I see here. If you feel the same way about me, I would be willing to consider your strongest offer."*

Holdout Example 2

Employer: *"Ms. Johnson, we are impressed with your credentials and would like you to be a contributing member of our team. What kind of compensation package do you have in mind?"*

Candidate: *"Mr. Thompson, I am truly flattered; thank you. I am very interested in this position and know we can work well together. Exactly what do you have in mind?"*

Go-with-the-Flow Example 1

Employer: *"Mr. Smith, what salary are you seeking?"*

Candidate: *"Well, Mr. Jones, there are two reasons why I'm here today. I would be foolish to deny that money is very important, but financial considerations are secondary to securing the right job with the right company. I'm more interested in challenge and opportunity. There is room for negotiation, but according to my research, the salary for someone with my qualifications and value is in the neighborhood of $67,000 to $78,500. I would expect a salary within this range."*

Go-with-the-Flow Example 2

Employer: *"Ms. Johnson, we are impressed with your credentials and would like to have you as a part of our team. What salary do you have in mind?"*

Candidate: *"Mr. Thompson, I am truly flattered; thank you. I am very interested in this position and know we can work well together. I am currently earning $69,000 a year with a full benefit package. For me to make a move, and based on my perceived value to your company, I would need a base salary of at least $75,000."*

Most people are uncomfortable with salary negotiating and even more uncomfortable about knowing when and where to incorporate it into the interview process. The longer the subject of money is avoided, the better it is for the candidate. The reasoning here is that you have had an opportunity to impress the employer with your résumé, perhaps over the telephone during a prescreening process and again at the interview.

Once you have survived all that and the employer calls you back for a second interview, you can be sure he or she is impressed. The employer is interested in you and what he or she believes you will bring to the company. At this point it probably would take a vast difference between what the employer wants to pay you to fill the position and what you want to receive for him or her to lose interest. You know you are within the salary range the employer will consider because of your preparation for the meeting.

TIPS

Here are some tips for negotiating your salary:

1. Don't bring up salary before the company initiates the discussion.
2. Do your research on what peers in that company earn and peers in other companies in that industry and in that geographic area earn.
3. Understand what you are worth.
4. Provide a range of salaries when asked, with a minimum you would accept.
5. Keep in mind that you may be worth more than you think. This is particularly true when large companies open new branch offices in your region.
6. Be careful not to undervalue your worth.
7. Overvalue your worth—you may even think you are irreplaceable to the employer.
8. Don't think the employer is in the driver's seat when it comes to negotiating salary.
9. Approach salary negotiations by assigning value to your qualifications and promises of performance.
10. Always think "self-funding."
11. Don't take the process personally. Salaries are assigned to your position, not to you.
12. Be prepared with industry and discipline research to support your negotiation.

13. You're more marketable when employed than when unemployed. Still try to deal from strength; don't fold your hand too quickly. However, you can't play "hard to get" when you have little or nothing to leverage.

14. Don't forget to include benefits as part of the compensation package.

15. Put emphasis on benefits rather than concentrating on the gross salary figure.

16. Project an image that is commensurate with the salary being negotiated.

17. To put a high price tag on yourself, provide support to justify the salary figure. That support may include previous W2s and your interviewing business plan.

18. State a specific figure on the résumé or in the cover letter.

19. Don't negotiate salary and benefits over the telephone if that can be avoided.

20. Try not to be too quick to accept an employer's first or second offer.

21. Use timing as a way to establish your value in the eyes of employers.

22. Do not fail to assess the employer's needs properly and develop a strategy to meet those needs as well as relate this strategy to your salary requirements.

23. Prep to ensure that you can handle the employer's salary questions and avoid saying the wrong thing.

24. Give yourself enough room to negotiate.

25. Know when to leave a job or company for opportunities somewhere else that will pay better.

26. Never lie about previous salaries. It's way too easy to verify.

Great Answers to Salary-Related Questions

- *What kind of salary are you looking for?*

  Attempt to get the company to make the first offer. Most negotiating professionals believe that whoever brings up salary first loses in the negotiating game. If possible, try to deflect the question so that you don't disclose a number first. The following is a gutsy but effective response.

  "We are all interested in making a good salary, but it is important for me to contribute and grow along with your company. Based on this interview and speaking with other employees at your company, I am very interested in working for Best Industries. If you feel the same way, I'd be very interested in entertaining your strongest offer."

- *What salary do you think you are worth?*

  You are looking for the highest possible starting salary, and the company is looking to hire you for the lowest possible cost. Try to determine the average salary for the position you are seeking in your geographic area. You do not want to bring up salary first, but if you need to give a figure, at least you'll be prepared.

  "I'm looking for a career opportunity where I can contribute and be compensated for my efforts. I believe I am well qualified for this job,

and I'm sure if you feel the same, you'll present me with a fair offer. May I ask the salary range for this position?"

- ### *What is your current salary?*

   What you earn now has no direct bearing on what you are worth or what you want to make, though it is difficult to support this in an interview without seeming defensive or awkward. Though the interviewer is looking for specifics, you can be somewhat elusive and general without compromising the quality of your response.

   "I am earning a base salary of $86,000 and have a full benefits package and three weeks of vacation a year. However, I don't believe this information will guide you in measuring my value for this position, since the two jobs are very different."

- ### *What is your salary history?*

   The interviewer is looking to build a historical picture of your salary over the years, including raises, percentage increases, and promotions. Try to deflect the question without answering it, as in this response.

   Response A: "Over the past 10 years I have received consistent promotions to positions of increasing responsibility, along with appropriate salary increases. One of my reasons for seeking a new position is that my current employer has standardized salary increases. I am a contributing force with the company and am not happy receiving the same increases as a person who does just enough to get by. I am looking for a situation where I am compensated for my specific, measurable contributions."

   Another approach would be to disengage the past from the future, as in this response.

   Response B: "Over the last 10 years I have received regular salary increases and promotions to positions of increasing responsibility. My current salary is in the low seventies, and the reason I am here is to improve on that. I enjoy my job and the people for whom I work. However, it is a very small, family-owned company, and my research leads me to believe that I can do much better financially with a larger company."

■ *What would you like to be earning five years from now?*

The interviewer is trying to gauge your ambitions. Maybe she or he is looking for an ambitious person who wants to become a millionaire. However, she or he may be searching for a candidate who will be happy to remain in one position, with minimal raises, for an extended period. This is a good time for honesty. You don't want to be stuck in a dead-end job when your goal is to earn millions, and you don't want the pressure of having to bite off more than you can chew if you are satisfied with less.

"I am an energetic peak performer who aspires to reach his full potential. I am an avid learner and one who thirsts for more and more responsibility. I would like to be earning as much income as possible, commensurate with my ability to contribute to organizational growth and profits."

■ *What is your minimum salary requirement?*

Beware of this question. Unless you are desperate, it should never be answered. If you know your minimum requirement and need the position, by all means provide the interviewer with a figure. Otherwise, inform the interviewer that your credentials, qualifications, and skills are above minimum salary standards.

"I am proud of my work history, my skills and qualifications, and the value I offer a prospective employer. I base my compensation solely on my ability to contribute to an organization's bottom line, not on a minimum salary requirement. I am very interested in pursuing a position with your firm, and if you are interested in hiring me, I would be willing to entertain your strongest offer."

■ *Why aren't you earning more than you currently earn?*

Be flattered and take it as a compliment. The interviewer is telling you that he or she feels you are worth more than you are getting. Provide a realistic answer that will not compromise your future earning potential with this company.

"During the last 11 years it was more important for me to work at a job with flexible hours so that I could spend time with my three children. I realize that I have compromised my earnings while raising my children. Now that they're all on their own, I am free to pursue a career with a salary commensurate with my abilities."

■ *How important are company benefits to you?*

Benefits are quite costly to companies these days, and unfortunately, a number of firms and organizations are selecting candidates on the basis of their ability to decline benefits. If benefits are absolutely necessary, say so but also mention that your salary is negotiable (if it is). If benefits are not essential, the following answer might be an effective one.

"I know that benefits are costly to companies these days. No, benefits are not essential, but a fair and equitable salary is."

■ *Have you ever been turned down for a salary increase?*

The interviewer is assuming that you have asked for one in the past. If you say yes, the interviewer may conclude that you may ask for raises between reviews, and this will turn him or her off. The best answer is no unless you have a story that unequivocally justifies your request for the raise.

"Yes. Three years ago I developed a warehouse tracking system that saved the company over $48,000 a year in payroll. I requested a raise based on my efforts and was refused. Instead, the company tendered me a one-time bonus check for $20,000."

■ *What is your total family income?*

The interviewer is probing beyond what is reasonable. Your family income has nothing to do with your value as a potential employee or the amount of money the company is willing to pay. Maybe the interviewer feels that if your spouse makes a good living, you'll accept less. At any rate, avoid answering this question unless for some reason you feel compelled to do so.

"I am an energetic individual who aspires to reach her full potential. I thirst for challenge, responsibility, and opportunity. I would like to earn as much as I possibly can, commensurate with my ability to contribute to organizational growth and profits. With all due respect, I don't believe my family income has any bearing on this."

The Hiring Proposal

IT IS ESSENTIAL to stay in touch with the hiring authority on a continuing basis after the interview. Be professional. The important thing to do during the follow-up stage is to reinforce and strengthen your image while keeping your candidacy at the forefront. Be aware of the fine line between remaining in contact and becoming a nuisance. Do not step over it, although that is hard to do. A watch may measure a job seeker's time frame, while that of the hiring authority is measured on a calendar.

Immediately after the interview (within 24 hours), send a thank-you note or letter. Mention that you appreciate the time the hiring manager spent with you and that you remain interested in the position, and define your understanding of the next scheduled contact (telephone call or meeting). Call to ask about the status of your application and the decision on the position if you have not heard anything after a week or 10 days. Review your notes from the meeting and look back at them before calling or corresponding with the company representative.

A highly effective method to keep your name in front of the hiring manager without being abrasive is to send a short e-mail with a compelling article or link pertinent to the industry. This concept is huge. You now have an excuse to bring something of interest to the hiring manager while disguising your motive somewhat. The hiring manager will get it, but the whole thing will come off better.

Still no answer from the hiring authority? No decision on the position? Devote your efforts to creating a *hiring proposal*.

Creating a Hiring Proposal

Sales Process	Interviewing Process
1. Identify prospects.	1. Target and identify prospective employers.
2. Contact the prospects and provide general information on the product or service.	2. Call for appointments and/or mail résumés.
3. Visit the prospects and make presentation.	3. Interview.
4. Attempt to close the deal on the spot.	4. Attempt to force a hiring decision at the end of the interview.
5. Write and send a formal proposal.	5. Write and send a hiring proposal, if appropriate.
6. Follow up.	6. Follow up.

The points above depict the similarity of the sales process and the job search process. You have progressed from point 1 to point 4 already. Still no answer? The next step in your sales program may be to write and send a hiring proposal.

The hiring proposal is highly effective, especially when:

- You feel you might not be the strongest candidate for the job.
- You have not been offered the job yet.
- The hiring process has been delayed.
- There are key points you need to make to offset the interviewer's objections that were raised during the interview.

> The hiring proposal is a formal written document forwarded to the hiring authority after an interview. This document offers your services to the company or organization. In effect, you are telling the prospective employer that *you have accepted it as your future employer.*

It is useful for proposing the creation of a new position that does not exist in the company but that you envision would benefit the organization directly. Under the right conditions, it is also used to reinforce a successful interview.

Make Them an Offer They Can't Refuse

Okay, it's a huge cliché, but it has some merit here. A hiring proposal is an innovative and effective method of showing initiative. Employers view spunk and initiative favorably. Those qualities show you are an enterprising individual, a take-charge proactive person.

In today's competitive job market, everyone must see himself or herself as self-employed. You should use every effective marketing tool to promote yourself to potential employers. A hiring proposal is similar to any other proposal. It is an effective promotional instrument that communicates the distinct advantages of the offer (you) and the benefits the company will receive.

Imagine a situation where you leave the interview certain you can handle the job responsibilities. However, you feel you were unable to get your message across as powerfully as you intended to. This is not the time to wait for a letter of rejection. Write a hiring proposal, making sure to cover your message powerfully in this document. A sample hiring proposal follows:

Randall Nobel

1234 8th Street
Fremont, MI 40002
(505) 555-6722

March 13, 2014

Mr. James Allen, President
JJ Allen & Company
123 32nd Place
Fremont, MI 44403

Dear Mr. Allen:

I truly enjoyed meeting with you and your employees last Tuesday, touring your plant, and discussing the position of warehouse systems administrator for JJ Allen & Company. You were a terrific host, and it was great meeting you and your group.

You spoke in depth of the need to centralize the purchasing done by JJ Allen & Company's five locations. Your personal goal of reducing inventory levels 20 percent while improving delivery schedules is admirable. I know I can be of assistance to you in attaining your objective.

It also appeared that senior management was seeking automated inventory-tracking solutions. In order to improve customer service, the development and installation of an effective inventory tracking system is mandatory. This aspect is one I handled at two of the three companies for which I worked.

I am so convinced that I can contribute immediately to JJ Allen & Company's goals, growth objectives, and current needs that I would like to offer my services to your firm on the following terms:

- I propose coming on board as an inventory control and purchasing subcontractor for a 90-day period. Within the first 30 days I will convert JJ Allen's current inventory software into a cutting-edge program. This will enable you to see a 20 percent reduction in inventory by the end of the third month, along with improvement of customer order shipments from 87 percent to a minimum of 95 percent—guaranteed!

- I will work with all satellite location buyers to centralize the purchasing department. This will eliminate duplication of orders and reduce high shipping fees, enabling you to lessen payroll costs. Within this 90-day time frame I will tighten up the purchasing process by reducing the prices we pay, improving the terms of our agreements, and showing an overall increase in productivity. Eliminating *location buyers* will allow us to train and reassign present buyers as inventory specialists, key personnel who will allow us to maintain low inventory levels while achieving near 100 percent service levels.

- I have had more than 7 years' experience in designing and implementing automated warehouses utilizing a computerized conveyor system. This conveyor system picks and tracks the inventory via computerized robotics. Although JJ Allen & Company may not need such a system for at least a year, I will submit to you (within this same 90-day period) an initial design for this system, along with the costs and the cost-benefits of this type of system. A consultant's fee for this project alone would run $25,000-plus.

Mr. Allen, I have worked in this profession for over 15 years and have a solid reputation, including strong endorsements from industry professionals. The best endorsement, however, would be for me to demonstrate to you that I am the best person for the job.

At the end of this 90-day period, our work will be groundbreaking for JJ Allen. During this 90-day period, we can assume my services on a contract basis. My commitment to your firm, along with my expertise and team-spirited management style, will enable us to discuss a permanent employment opportunity at that time. I am certain you will be impressed.

I will call you by the end of the week to discuss this further. I look forward to our next meeting.

Sincerely,
Randall Nobel

Preparing References for the Interview

TODD RECEIVED A terrific promotion that involved running a sales region for a Fortune 50 company. It was an internal promotion, and sometimes those are the most difficult to get. Once in a company, you often get stereotyped in a certain role and are kept there. It can be challenging to get others to see you where you see yourself. If you cannot relate to that, you need to get out more.

During the interview process Todd went for the close in the final interview with the vice president. The vice president said his only possible reservation about Todd was how he might work with the many cross-functional groups the position required. Todd instinctively knew what to do: he rallied his colleagues and internal sponsors.

Todd gathered one person from each of five different disciplines within the company, mostly people whom he knew or who had some name recognition. Each one called the vice president and got his voice mail. Their messages were scripted to address how well Todd worked with each group despite the fact that he came from a different discipline.

The vice president made the offer about 10 days later. For the next year, whenever that vice president, Mike, would introduce him, he would follow with a joke about the assault reference campaign that Todd launched to address his objection. I'm not sure Todd would have gotten that job had he not done that. For the record, he also completed an interviewing business plan like the one in Chapter 19.

What Is an Endorsement?

Webster's New World Dictionary defines the word *reference* as "the giving of the name of another person who can offer information or recommendation; referring or being referred." A reference attests to what you have done in the past.

For the word *endorsement* it reads "a statement, as in an advertisement, that one approves of a product or service; to give approval to; support; sanction." An endorsement promotes a candidate to a prospective employer in anticipation of that candidate's future production capabilities.

You might consider the difference between a reference and an endorsement subtle, but it is not. References attest; endorsements promote. There can be no doubt that endorsements are powerful sales tools in many market segments. However, seldom has the concept of endorsements been used in securing a career opportunity. Endorsements are an important component of a job search campaign.

An employment endorsement is similar to the concept of celebrity recommendations of a product or service. If basketball superstar Michael Jordan appeared on television and said that Nike basketball sneakers worked well for him, you might be impressed. However, if he implied that they not only worked for him but would work equally well for you, it would entice you to be like Mike. This would prompt you to purchase Nike footgear because it would make you feel you could play nearly as well as him. You would be impressed by his endorsement.

It added that extra degree of credibility to entice you to visit the store for a closer look at the product. It was instrumental in persuading you to purchase the product. In much the same way, a solid employment endorsement communicates to a prospective employer that you will meet his or her needs and assist him or her in solving organizational problems. And it is based on a credible source other than you.

Those selected to provide your endorsements are in reality your sponsors—not a sponsor in terms of monetary sponsorship but one who believes in you and supports your overall efforts. These individuals will provide you with one of the most potent weapons in your job search arsenal.

You have invested a lot of time and resources to get this interview, your next job is within reach, and it appears that everything is about to come together for you. But your references are weak or blasé and perhaps include contradictory comments. If this is the case, strong endorsements can enhance your chance of winning the job.

The Endorsement Portfolio

Whether an employer reaches out to references or not, a professional endorsement portfolio powerfully supports your job search campaign right from the start. If you promote your references as endorsements, it's possible that your list of endorsements-references will not even need to be corroborated. An endorsement portfolio is a set of four to six letters from business and professional associates describing your skills, abilities, qualifications, and value backed by quantifiable data and information, promoting you to a potential employer. Ideally, the makeup of this group would be:

- *Two superiors.* Promoting your value (ability to perform, produce, and contribute to organizational goals). They certify your support of organizational goals.
- *One peer.* Endorsing your ability to work as a team member and leader. This person confirms your ability to put organizational needs before your personal agenda.
- *One subordinate.* Vouching for your training and coaching skills. This endorsement also promotes your supervisory skills.
- *Two major clients/vendors.* Affirming your high-quality customer service and professional integrity.

If you are employed, obtaining an endorsement from anyone associated with your current employer may be a challenge. If you worked for firms that have gone out of business or were purchased by another company, you may find it difficult to obtain endorsements. In these and other cases you must depend heavily on your imagination and creative resources to construct an alternative plan that meets the criteria of endorsement marketing.

You may wish to pursue former superiors and peers for endorsements. Those you worked with previously are an excellent source for testimonials. Although recent endorsements are best, it is better to have past endorsements than none at all. The main objective is to develop a portfolio of endorsements from people who unequivocally can promote your skills and abilities—your value.

Many people leave a job and break all ties with their superiors and peers as well as with the organization. A word of caution is called for here. Do not burn bridges! For whatever reason you depart, you must swallow your pride, file away your ego, and consider the termination no-fault, thus allowing you to approach people for endorsements. You need to leave with your head held high. Do not depart on a sour note, but if you have already done so, mend fences!

If you make a concerted and genuine effort, most former bosses, peers, and subordinates will support you and offer you an endorsement. In their book *Job Search—The Total System*, Kenneth Dawson and Sheryl Dawson make it clear what strategy you must adopt to obtain the all-important endorsement:

> *Never write off your relationship with your ex-boss until you've given your best shot at getting a reference. And note that your best shot doesn't mean one phone call or a perfunctory inquiry through his [her] secretary. It means professional persistence and courteous insistence that you expect nothing less [than the endorsement].*

Who Writes the Endorsement Letter?

The endorsement letter describes your skills, abilities, qualifications, past performance, contributions, and character. It is possible that the words used will not be compatible with the direction in which you are heading. Here is an example.

Bob, a branch manager of a community bank, was downsized after a bank merger. His primary responsibilities had been the daily management and operations of the branch. He realized he thoroughly enjoyed sales and marketing. He also knew he was instrumental in improving the bank's core deposits. He decided to seek a sales and marketing opportunity.

Bob's former boss provided him with a letter of reference. The letter mentioned that Bob was a highly skilled manager, worked well supervising employees, and had a solid aptitude for finances and budgeting. These were very nice references but poor endorsements for Bob's pursuit of a sales position. What Bob needs is an endorsement emphasizing his mastery of marketing and sales. His former boss should highlight how, as a result of Bob's efforts, bank core deposits grew 17 percent a year in the highly competitive banking environment. Bob's endorsement letter must promote his proficiency at customer relations and his strong negotiating and closing skills, all of which are critical to landing a position in sales.

The people selected to endorse you may need a little coaching. The more enthusiastic your endorsers are, the more exciting the message they will convey to prospective employers. Make them cognizant of the path you are taking and the skills you need reinforced in their letters. Coach them!

Caution is also advised in regard to the writing skills of the person you ask for a reference. Many executives who can sell, manufacture, distribute, and do a host of other things cannot write a letter. Consider drafting a letter yourself. Superstars don't write the endorsements they make; the product manufacturer or advertising agency does. It is also possible that you will need the document before they get around to writing it. Ask them if they mind your drafting a letter for their signature or at least offer them a template of ideas. Some people are glad to have you take the responsibility off their hands. By the way, make sure your own writing skills are excellent before attempting this task.

10 Steps for Obtaining Endorsements

1. Identify four to six people to provide you with powerful endorsements.
2. Contact all of them and request that they agree to promote your job search efforts.
3. Receive permission to write the endorsement yourself.
4. Write the endorsement, linking the information to the résumé.
5. Bring or send the letter to the endorser for review and signature.
6. Have the endorser send the endorsement back to you on his or her letterhead (company or personal).
7. Photocopy the endorsements (enough copies to match the number of résumés you have prepared for distribution).
8. Bring or mail a thank-you note to the endorser along with a manila folder. Inside the folder should be a copy of your résumé and a copy of the endorsement letter. Request that the folder be kept handy for reference calls. In that way the endorser is prepared to promote you in an empowering way with every call.
9. After every interview contact your endorsers and coach them on your focus for when this particular employer calls. It does not matter if this is done by phone, fax, e-mail, or in person; the important thing is to communicate after every interview.
10. Regardless of the number of interviews you have, maintain contact with your endorsers at least once a month. Always be certain that you have current addresses, phone numbers, and fax numbers.

Sample Endorsement Portfolio

1. Mr. Greg Fantin, President
   United Office Supply
   123 Mileta Avenue,
   Burlington, MA 01777
   (617) 555-0000
2. Ms. Susan Cooper, VP Operations
   United Office Supply
   123 Mileta Avenue
   Burlington, MA 01777
   (617) 555-0000
3. Mr. Rich Panek, Sales Manager
   United Office Supply
   123 Mileta Avenue
   Burlington, MA 01777
   (617) 555-0000
4. Ms. Michelle David, Warehouse Manager/Inventory Control
   United Office Supply
   123 Mileta Avenue
   Burlington, MA 01777
   (617) 555-0000
5. Mr. Justin Darland, VP Sales Xerox Corporation
   2300 Xerox Place
   Waltham, MA 01116
   (617) 555-1122
6. Pat Rush, President Portland Pen Co., Inc.
   99 Vannah Avenue
   Portland, ME 01566
   (207) 555-9977

Sample Endorsement Letters

United Office Supply
123 Mileta Avenue
Burlington, MA 01777
(617) 555-0000

August 10, 20___

To Whom It May Concern:

Any company fortunate enough to have Sandy Haynes as warehouse manager has a true advantage in today's highly competitive economic climate. UOS has benefited from Mr. Haynes's expertise in management and employee and customer relations for 12 years. His independent management style allowed UOS to grow 480 percent over a 12-year period, and Sandy kept his warehouse operations one step ahead of the rest of the competition.

His ability to anticipate and quickly adjust to changing technologies has resulted in contributions to corporate profits in the millions of dollars during his tenure with UOS.

We all but begged him to relocate to our new headquarters, but he felt that relocation to Chicago would not be in the best interest of his family. He did, however, spend two months in the Windy City training his replacement.

A true professional, Sandy Haynes is an indispensable asset to any organization. His team leadership skills, together with his visionary expertise, are unparalleled. Please feel free to contact me personally should you require any further information.

Sincerely,

Greg Fantin
President

United Office Supply
123 Mileta Avenue
Burlington, MA 01777
(617) 555-0000

August 18, 20___

To Whom It May Concern:

I had the pleasure of working with Sandy Haynes over the past six years as his immediate superior. His analytical approach, technical expertise, and aptitude for anticipating and reacting to changing environments are unmatched. He has a special knack for taking preemptive measures in eliminating problems to allot more time planning as opposed to putting out fires.

When you hire Sandy Haynes, not only do you hire a competent management professional, but you employ a man who is loved and respected by all. He gives credit to his team, tactfully corrects errors, and generates excitement, energy, and cooperation among team members. Like any true superstar, he brings out a person's best so that everyone can share in triumphs and challenges together.

In closing, those of us at UOS will miss him and always remember him. Sandy made an impact on everyone he came in contact with nationwide. Allow him to impact your company. I only hope we will not have to compete against him in the future. Feel free to contact me at home at any time regarding this endorsement (617-555-8822).

Sincerely,

Susan Cooper
VP Operations

United Office Supply
123 Mileta Avenue
Burlington, MA 01777
(617) 555-0000

August 29, 20___

To Whom It May Concern:

As regional sales manager for UOS, responsible for annual revenues exceeding $50 million, I can say with absolute certainty that the lifeline for our reputation and growth is customer service. The speed and accuracy of the delivery of products to our clients determines our success, and that depends on efficient warehouse operations.

I have worked with Sandy Haynes for over eight years. There is no greater team player when it comes to any type of management. He listens to all parties concerned, sees the big picture, and has the confidence and foresight to integrate everyone's ideas to come up with a comprehensive plan that works for the company. He will sacrifice his own beliefs when it comes to the good of the company. However, that does not happen often because he has such an exacting pulse on the industry specifically and on economics and business in general.

I highly endorse Mr. Sandy Haynes. We lost him as our warehouse manager but will never lose him as a friend.

Sincerely,

Rich Panek
Sales Manager

United Office Supply
123 Mileta Avenue
Burlington, MA 01777
(617) 555-0000

August 29, 20___

To Whom It May Concern:

I was hired by Mr. Haynes in 1983. In the 12 interviews I went on, Mr. Haynes was the most professional, trustworthy, and honest hiring manager I confronted. He explained to me the pros and the cons of the job and explicitly stated what he expected in the short and long term. He also clearly noted that he was there to train, develop, and coach us all to success.

Little did I know that 10 years later I would be promoted and become the first female warehouse manager in the history of the company. Sandy encouraged me to be the best I could be and taught me to think on my feet and strategically plan for the future. I owe my success to Sandy Haynes. He is a firm, tough, and demanding manager yet fair, open, and motivating.

I know of no better mentor for our department. He made work challenging, fun, and exciting. As his replacement, I can only hope that my subordinates will feel half the respect and affection for me that we felt for him.

Sincerely,

Michelle David
Warehouse Manager/Inventory Control

Xerox Corporation
2300 Xerox Place
Waltham, MA 01116
(617) 555-1122

April 29, 20___

To Whom It May Concern:

We have had the pleasure of associating with Sandy Haynes over the past 14 years with UOS and Grand Mountain Office Distributors. In my 30-plus years in the business, all with Xerox, I have never met a more professional, talented, or personable warehouse manager.

He is a strong and formidable negotiator. He always has the best interest of his company at heart. He is fair and always looks for a win-win solution in any negotiation.

He is a loyal and dedicated professional who will enhance any company. His value, when measured against that of his peers, is truly head and shoulders above the rest. Xerox will be pleased to provide you with any additional information you need. Contact me at the above address, and I will quickly respond to your inquiries.

Sincerely,

Justin Darland
VP Sales

Portland Pen Co., Inc.

99 Vannah Avenue
Portland, ME 01566
(207) 555-9977

May 12, 20___

To Whom It May Concern:

Portland Pen began operations in 1992 with zero sales. We had a new marketing concept that was different from anything existing on the market at that time. Most people resist change—not Sandy Haynes. He listened to our ideas, added some of his own, and, as a result, was instrumental in assisting Portland Pen to reach its current market position as a $6 million company poised to go international and positioned for explosive growth.

At a time when Sandy Haynes could have enjoyed the relationships he had with other firms, he saw he could maintain those relations while opening new markets. He got the president of his company to look at our program, negotiated a highly profitable arrangement for Grand Mountain Office Distributors, and gave us a chance. Today, Grand Mountain Office Distributors sells over $125,000 of our product and has given us credibility in the market.

Sandy saw the benefit to his customer and his company. He is a man of his word, a man of integrity, and a bottom-line progressive management professional. He helped make Portland Pen what it is today and what it will be tomorrow. Anyone who hires him is truly fortunate to experience his professionalism.

Sincerely,

Pat Rush
President

Acknowledgments

We would like to thank McGraw-Hill for partnering with us on this and all of our other books. Specifically, Dannalie Diaz was a big help in this second edition and in working with us line by line on the final manuscript, and Janice Race, as our editing supervisor, demonstrated exceptional attention to detail. Thanks to both of you!

Michael and Jay

Index

About the Authors

Jay Block is an industry pioneer and one of the nation's leading motivational career and empowerment coaches. He is the author of 18 career and motivational books, 12 of which are published by McGraw-Hill. Jay is a highly respected trainer and keynote presenter and is best known for combining world-class motivational techniques with cutting-edge job campaign tools and strategies that result in rapid success. He works with job seekers who are unemployed, underemployed, unhappily employed, and happily employed wanting to advance. Jay developed seven international certification programs for career coaches and trainers, including his award-winning program, Five Steps to Rapid Employment™. In addition, he created the first-ever interview coaching certification (CEIP) for the Professional Association of Résumé Writers and Career Coaches that today remains the industry standard for successful interviewing strategies.

Jay travels the country to share his ideas and concepts with job seekers and employment professionals. He lives in South Florida and can be reached by visiting his website at www.jayblock.com.

Michael Betrus grew up in Michigan and graduated from Michigan State University, majoring in accounting. Michael is a sales director by trade with a Fortune 500 company. He has authored or coauthored a number of books on résumés, cover letters, executive recruiters, and, of course, interviewing, all published by McGraw-Hill. Having conducted much primary research on these topics as well as interviewed and hired hundreds of candidates, Michael brings a unique, street-smart perspective on the career transition process. He lives in Texas and has one son, Michael, who balances a passion for his academics with his desire to play in the major leagues one day.